LEARN YOUR LIFE PURPOSE

Happiness Now for the Miracle-Minded

Linda L. Chappo,
Author and Spiritual Midwife

Copyright©2024 by Linda L.Chappo

Published in the United States by "Pinnacle of Success Books"

Trade Paperback ISBN: 978-0-9966895-6-4

Cover art by Klassic Designs/99 Designs

Visit Linda online at www.HearttoHeartLiving.com

www.LearnYourLifePurpose.com

All rights reserved. No part of this book maybe reproduced by any mechanical, photographic, electronic process, or in the form of a phonographic record; nor may it be stored in the retrieval system, transmitted, or otherwise be copied for public or private use - other than for 'fair use' as brief quotations embodied in articles and reviews - without prior written permission of the author.

The author of this book does not dispense medical advice or prescribe the use of any technique as a form of treatment for physical, emotional, or medical problems without the advice of a physician, either directly or indirectly. The intent of the author is only to offer information of a general nature to help you in your quest for emotional and Spiritual well-being. In the event you use any of the information in this book for yourself, the author and the publisher assume no responsibility for your actions.

"All ACIM quotes are from the Third Edition of A Course in Miracles"

copyright ©2007 by the Foundation for Inner Peace

448 Ignacio Blvd., #306, Novato, CA 94949

* I would like to express my gratefulness to The Foundation for Inner Peace, Tam Morgan, and Deborah Roberts, Chief International & Communications Officer, Foundation for Inner Peace for permission to use the quotes from A Course in Miracles.

Foundation for Inner Peace: Since 1975, the Foundation for Inner Peace is a non-profit organization dedicated to publishing, distributing, and discussing A Course in Miracles. To learn more about A Course in Miracles, I recommend you visit the website of the scribe-authorized publisher and copyright holder, the Foundation for Inner Peace (www.acim.org).

The Foundation's website has a wide variety of Course-related materials, including biographies and photos of the scribes, a completely searchable online Web Edition of A Course in Miracles, free access to daily lessons in five languages, audio recordings, study guide, information about the many ACIM translations, access to podcasts and webinars, as well as mobile apps. The Foundation also donates thousands of copies of ACIM.

The organization depends on donations to fulfill its mission. If you would like to support more people to benefit from A Course in Miracles, donating to the Foundation for Inner Peace would be a worthy endeavor. Thank you.

Dedication

"My utmost gratitude to Jesus/Holy Spirit of A.C.I.M. for guiding me along this journey."

Other books by Linda L. Chappo

- The Art of Listening to Your Heart and Soul: Awaken to Your Intuition and Divine Inner Guidance
- How to Handle Change and Uncertainty—due in 2025
- Marry Yourself First: Your Key to Manifesting Loving Relationships
- Weigh Less Express: Six Sure Fire Ways to Your Ideal Weight, Better Health, and an Empowered Life
- The Thirteen Deadly Mistakes that Can Destroy a Woman's First Business: When Failure is Not an Option
- A Romance and Dating Journal: For Mastering Your Romantic Journey
- A Return to Noah's Arc: Finding a Better Way – The Untold Story (A children's book in 5 languages)

TABLE OF CONTENTS

PREFACE 7
INTRODUCTION 8
CHAPTER ONE: YOUR TRANSFORMATIVE JOURNEY 12
    The Path to Purpose and Passion is Often Like a Maze! 14
    Shift to Illumination 14
    Fuel for Your Soul 16
    Put Your Passion Into Perspective 17
    Label Your Life Journey 18
CHAPTER TWO: QUESTION EVERYTHING! 23
    Seven Critical Life Questions 24
CHAPTER THREE: IT'S TIME TO COURSE-CORRECT 30
    Build a Better Mindset 32
    Shift Forward by Identifying Triggers 34
CHAPTER FOUR: BECOME MIRACLE-MINDED! 37
    Shift to a Limitless Life Path: Seven Steps to Freedom 39
    Create A New Pattern 41
CHAPTER FIVE: TAKE IT UP A NOTCH 43
    Enter a New Paradigm 43
    Destined for Greatness 44
    Create Powerful Intentions 45
CHAPTER SIX: EMBRACE THE POSSIBILITIES 54
CHAPTER SEVEN: THE AMAZING POWERS OF YOUR MIND 57
    Own Your Superpowers: Awaken to Your Intuition and Imagination ... 61
CHAPTER EIGHT: THE A.R.T. OF INNER LISTENING 66
    Set Your Cornerstone 67

Six Takeaways from The A.R.T. of LISTENING! 69

Listening Equals Inner Strength 74

CHAPTER NINE: GOAL-DIRECTED MEDITATION 76

Lighten Your Emotional & Mental Burdens 77

Three Ways to Activate Your Goals 81

Three Approaches to Your Goal-directed Practice 85

Access Your Levels of Mind 89

CHAPTER TEN: DREAMS—YOUR SACRED GATEWAY 93

Dreams as Spiritual Significance 94

Take Your Dreams Seriously 97

Dreams: A Gateway to Your Power, Passion, and Purpose! 97

Dreams as an Entryway to Your Future 100

Trust in the Process 102

CHAPTER ELEVEN: ALIGN WITH YOUR HIGHER POWER 104

Do You Have Free Will or Not —The Script is Written 110

CHAPTER TWELVE: CO-CREATE YOUR IDEAL LIFE PATH 116

Three Reasons You Don't Take Action on Your Dreams 118

What I Know For Sure! 119

Develop Your Inner Resources 123

CHAPTER THIRTEEN: THE PROCESS OF DISCOVERY 128

Honor Your Life Experiences 129

Access Your Inner Genius 131

Imagine Your Mind on Daydreams and Fantasies! 132

Discover Your Ideal Life Path 137

Your Soul Speaks of Your Destiny—Your Higher Ideal 137

Point #1: Mine Your Past for Clues 138

Point #2: Mine Your Present for Clues 141

Point #3: Mine Your Future for Clues 143

Chart Your Course 146

Everyone Has a Purpose 148

CHAPTER FOURTEEN: THE CHANGING PATH 149

Clarity Equals Your Turning Point 150

Take Solid Steps Toward Your Dreams 154

Look for Signposts to Stay on Course 157

CHAPTER FIFTEEN: LIVE YOUR PURPOSEFUL LIFE 161

Remember Your Wise Internal Resources 163

The Power of Your Personal Values 165

Brainstorm Your Way to Happiness Now 167

How Guidance Works 173

CHAPTER SIXTEEN: READJUST YOUR HALO 175

Part One: Be Miracle-Minded for Yourself 177

Remove the Wall From Around Your Heart 180

Part Two: Tap Into Energetic Vibrations 183

Part Three: Be Miracle-Minded in Your Relationships 186

Relationships as Mirrors 188

Co-create the Best Version of Yourself 189

Attract More Love and Friendships 190

Part Four—Be Miracle-Minded for Freedom 193

Suffering is Not an Option 195

Part Five—Empower Yourself 198

Utilize Your Superpowers 198

Tell Yourself a Different Story 198

PREFACE

As a personal growth expert and Spiritual midwife with years of professional healing service, I'm thrilled and humbled to guide you to birth the Divine seed of your life purpose. My intention is to help you grow, learn, and experience a true connection between your higher Self and your outer life that may bring you Happiness Now.

I'll encourage and support you in exploring your own internal landscape, and awaken your curiosity, creativity, and critical gifts. Think of it as your next big adventure or even the next surprising chapter in your most incredible life. Together we can forge a powerful new path for you to experience a present and a future of meaning, destiny, and a sense of purpose.

Your life will shift and change over time and when it does, trust me on this, you're still on course. It may sometimes seem like a painful detour. Always remember that this is the world of change. Every situation or circumstance will eventually shift and morph into some other kind of experience. I encourage you to get comfortable with change because it's a given and the more you go with the flow rather than fight it, the happier and more peaceful you'll be. You've taken the first step to making a shift toward happiness by deciding to follow your Dream or Learn Your Life Purpose. Let the adventure begin!

INTRODUCTION

You and I both live with the Big Mystery of Life ... and continue to ask those big life questions: "Why am I here? What am I here to do, be, have, and learn?"

You have lots of options for learning what you're destined to do for yourself and the world. This particular option is focused on how to develop your Spiritual awareness so you can learn your life purpose and more from your Higher Power and/or higher Self. No guessing from your ego, no errors through second hand suggestions, and no mucking around! If you really want clarity on your life, there's no better place to get it than directly from your Higher Power!

This coaching program is part memoir and part personal development coaching. I'll take you along a proven journey and show you how you too can learn your life purpose, as I did, and how listening to a Divine Inner Voice makes for a surprising, adventurous, and fulfilling life.

My greatest gift to you is for you to learn and experience the truth of who you are and how developing your awareness is a lifelong gift to yourself. Take my stories to heart and know that no matter where you are in your life, what you've experienced, or where you think you're going, it's all part of the life-enriching journey planned for you by the One who has your best interests in mind.

I'll assume you're already Miracle-Minded or believe in a metaphysical thought system. If so, then these ideas will not seem strange to you. They're right in alignment with what you believe in your heart and soul.

If you're a longtime *A Course in Miracles* student, you'll find that this program is not meant to be a serious study of ACIM. I call it ACIM-Lite. It's more like an introduction than a complex, long-winded interpretation. If you want the details, then please read the book. I've cherry-picked ACIM principles to support this program and implemented them to lead readers to their own personal transformation. I chose certain passages because they support my personal experiences. You don't have to know or even study *A Course in Miracles* to get value from this book.

INTRODUCTION

If you agree with the idea that a simple shift in perception can take you miraculously from a fearful perspective to one of love and acceptance, then you may be Miracle-Minded.

Let's be clear, *A Course In Miracles* is not a religion, but a Spiritual path or discipline. It came about in the 1960's and was designed as a Spiritual solution for workplace conflict. A research psychologist in an academic setting made it her goal to find a better way to get along with co-workers. The psychologist's Inner Voice, which she was told was Jesus, guided her to receive His training. Whether you believe that or not isn't important. These powerful teachings stand on their own. ACIM encourages a more modern approach to a happy and miraculous life ... one of freedom from guilt, suffering, and disconnection. After three decades I can attest to its amazing ability to change your life, work, and relationships!

You're reading this book today because you have a Dream, want to Learn Your Life Purpose, and you might self-identify as: "Spiritual, Metaphysical, or Miracle-Minded!" Because you're metaphysically minded you already have two important skills that apply to your purpose. They'll make it easier to achieve your miraculous new life.

1. You may have experienced breakthrough thinking, (going beyond the traditional thought systems). This means you're a natural born explorer. You challenge the traditional thought systems that place limits on consciousness.

2. You're courageous enough to know that there's more to this world than what you can experience with your five senses. And that puts you in a powerful position.

You might be wondering, *"Why did I design my life purpose coaching specifically for metaphysical and Miracle-Minded people?"* I did that because I know you and you're just like me. You're open-minded, heart centered, maybe empathic, and you may already be devoted to your Higher Power and focused consciousness. You've studied the Law of Attraction. You might believe in angel helpers and Spirit Guides who are all working towards a Divine Plan for our world.

You know the highly popular works of Deepak Chopra, Dr. Wayne Dyer, Marianne Williamson, and many others in the realm of personal growth and transformation. So you're at least one step ahead of everyone else. You and I believe in the quote, *"With God all things are possible."* As a self-proclaimed Spiritual Midwife, my mission is to help you birth your highest ideal of yourself and what you're destined to do or achieve.

On some level, you have an awareness of your Spiritual connection, but haven't been able to access it in a way that is transformational. I'm asking you not to lose faith, but to trust in the process. Your Higher Power has a plan for you and if you want to be in alignment with it: prepare yourself, do your part, and let go of control.

I realize that if you're unhappy with your career or life, you've not connected with that sacred seed within you. It's time to explore, discover, and birth what you think of as your Dream, Purpose, Passion, Calling, Mission, or Vision. That awareness means everything, can open doors, and change your life from mediocre to miraculous. And it might just come down to having a belief in the process and faith in yourself.

I currently see a trend toward 'evidence-based' material, particularly in health-related studies. The only 'evidence' in metaphysical knowledge is in the personal experience itself. Thousands, perhaps even millions of books and lectures describe the profound healings, successes, and miracles of metaphysical thought and implementation.

We know that miraculous change doesn't happen in a vacuum. If you believe in a Higher Power, have had some experience with conscious manifestation, and know there's something more for you, then that's proof enough.

That's why Learning Your Life Purpose appeals to the Miracle-Minded. You have an inner calling, like I do, and you're open minded enough to learn from one who has already done it, to go beyond what you already know.

You might be asking, *"well, Linda, how long will it take?"* My answer is this: *"It takes as long as it takes,"* depending on the plan for your life and your willingness to give it birth. I'll talk about that, and the thoughts and perceptions that may speed things up for you.

You'll learn a totally different perspective on Learning Your Life Purpose that other life purpose teachers are not touching on, and it'll contribute more to your peace and happiness than anything else I can teach you!

This is an experiential guide ... inviting you to participate in the Tools for Personal Growth. If you read through them without participating, it'll limit your experience. So, participate in the program to get the most benefits from it.

The Process of Discovery is designed to reveal what you're here to do, be, have, or learn. From that point on it's "open season" (transformational) on your awareness, consciousness, and experiences. In other words, *"All Heaven breaks loose for you!"*

I'll be teaching you about living your Dreams from a Spiritual or metaphysical perspective. You'll awaken to the birthright within you that may not only change your life, but the lives of those you interact with.

If you're ready to take the most important steps to realizing your Dreams and Learning Your Life Purpose, then read on and let's get a jumpstart on your happiness and fulfillment! May all the best come to you in leaps and bounds!

CHAPTER ONE

YOUR TRANSFORMATIVE JOURNEY

> *"When truly and finally you are living from the inside out, you will never again be susceptible to being upside down."* Jayem Hammer, author of "The Way of Mastery"

Welcome to *"Learn Your Life Purpose,"* the first part of a transformative journey designed to help you uncover the deeper meaning and direction in your life. As a personal growth expert, I am thrilled to guide you on this profound exploration of self-discovery, connecting you with your inner landscape, aligning you with your Higher Power, and embracing your authentic Self. I trust that it's evident to you that for your current life to become your Life Purpose, a shift is necessary.

Three stars are true stories from my own or an interviewee's personal experience.

*** **Take a Pause**—It was 1994 and I was in my first career transition after moving to San Francisco. Instead of quickly trying to figure out my next steps, I took a pause to lick my wounds, so to speak. After two and half years I closed my healing arts practice. I spent a lot of money, time, and effort on my Holistic Health education, private office, and marketing ... and I was good at what I did. Something just clicked for me that this career had become frustrating and unworkable. I initially felt that holistic healing was my Life Purpose, so I felt crushed!

Over time I realized my private practice wasn't going as well as I had envisioned and honestly ... I felt lost and confused. I share my story as a "finding your ideal career path situation!"

As I began thinking about my next steps I realized I had three advantages in my favor: a strong clairaudient ability, an expanded awareness through my meditation practice, and the mind-training program of *A Course in Miracles,* and its ability to instill in me a foundation for inner peace!

I immediately received an important clue ... clear inner guidance. My story is actually the exact opposite of how most people make a career decision. The difference is that I allowed my Miracle-Mind to lead me. In this situation my inner guidance came first, my curiosity came second, letting go came third, and passion came last.

My intuition was subtly directing me through repetitive and non-intrusive thoughts to visit a nearby college. I'd never gone to college, so the idea intrigued me. Then my inner guidance was clear ... I heard the word "typography." I had no idea what that was until I drove to a nearby college and discovered it was a class in the Graphic Communications department. Typography is the design or selection of letterforms to be organized into words and sentences eventually printed on a page.

Because of the 1) guidance, 2) my curiosity, and 3) the potential I saw in the graphic arts course, I instantly became enthusiastic about the program. Synchronistically, the very day I drove to the college to investigate typography, they were enrolling students for the new semester. Imagine that!

It was the mid 1990's when the graphic design program was switching from designing graphics by hand to using the Mac computer. So I had a lot of learning to do. I initially wondered how this would help me achieve the Vision I experienced a year and a half before? I decided to be patient and follow guidance. It didn't take long for me to discover that computer graphics would become 4) my passion! I loved it and continue to use those skills almost on a daily basis ... both as a writer, artist, and entrepreneur.

In order to follow my Higher Power's directions, I took part time classes and also worked part time until I graduated from college. Incase you were wondering about my next step after graduation, I didn't even have to apply for the job I wanted. My prospective employer came to me and offered me the perfect position.

The mental pause I took while in transition served me well. I made my way through the maze and found the treasure. It was all about NOT taking control, but allowing my Higher Power to lead me.*

The Path to Purpose and Passion is Often Like a Maze!

In today's fast-paced world, it's all too common to feel lost, disconnected, or unfulfilled. It's like being trapped in a maze with no clear direction on how to get out. Clarity is your goal for Learning Your Life Purpose and a way of the maze of disappointment and pain.

There are three areas of life that often bring the most pain: your service to the world (your work/career), your service to each other (your relationships), and your service to yourself (how you handle change via your emotions/perceptions). I'll address all three areas.

There is one area that brings the most satisfaction and joy to your life: that's when you consciously shift out of the maze and shift into an alignment with your Higher Power's plan for your happy life.

Shift to Illumination

You may experience workplace disappointment and struggle to find genuine satisfaction in your daily pursuits. But fear not, for this coaching program is here to illuminate the path towards a more purposeful and happier future.

You may have to think differently, like I did, to achieve your ideal career situation! You've most likely heard the following encouragement, *"Follow your bliss or passion"* and doors will open for you. Is that really the best advice for everyone? I don't think so. I believe one should start with a CLEAR and OPEN MIND, then listen to and follow your higher guidance ... leading to open doors and your Spirit-inspired passion.

Like you, I've traveled through an interesting maze to find my purpose. You've read my story of how I initially followed my passion as a holistic health counselor. Although it didn't work out as planned ... thinking differently by following my guidance provided a shift toward a better passion and more happiness!

WHY IS THIS IMPORTANT?

Many people enjoy their professions but some find their particular work or work relationships to be challenging. Statistics say that 77% of college graduates don't work in their chosen field and 40% don't love what they do.

You eventually become disenchanted with your career for primarily two reasons:

1. You don't like the work/field you thought you were initially passionate about. If you don't like the work, it's probably not your Life Purpose... unless you start over with a different mindset or change your mind about its place in your life.

2. You can't stand your co-workers or managers. You may not feel valued. In some cases both reasons cause you to quit and/or change occupations. In a later chapter you'll meet Daniela, a woman who didn't feel valued in her position. It just "clicked" for her one day, and you too may have heard that "click!"

Make a shift and travel a different path to defy the statistics. Instead of trying to figure it out as you go along, know that years of valuable time are quickly passing you by. Defy the statistics by choosing the new paradigm that puts you in a position of power, not powerlessness. The next new paradigm shift begins for you in "Chapter Five: Take it Up a Notch." First, there is work to do ... by using the Tools for Your Personal Growth. Personal growth starts and multiplies itself when you build a more meaningful future: correct your perceptions and make better decisions.

Give Birth to Your Sacred Seed Within

I believe everyone is born with a Sacred Seed (of destiny) implanted by your Higher Power. It's inside you, waiting for your attention. As you plant a seed into the earth for a particular result: a tree that eventually provides flowers, fruit, shade, joy, and greenery, your sacred Spirit-inspired seed also flowers your future with unending joy through life enrichment.

Giving birth to your Sacred Seed and/or your special Dream can be exciting. It's exciting because you may have thought and fantasized about your Dream(s) for a long time. As someone who is Miracle-Minded, you probably visualized it in detail, created positive and compelling affirmations, and maybe even felt your success.

It goes something like this: you see your efforts working. You stand on stage with your award. You finally got the raise for work well done. There's a line out the door of your new restaurant. Everyone signed up for your workshop and also bought your book! Your precious children are healthy, successful, and happy.

Allow your joy (real or imagined) to catapult you past any hurdles that might hold you back. Keep your Spirit-inspired goals in the forefront of your mind and keep taking those baby steps, like children do when they're first learning to walk.

Surprising and delightful experiences occur once you're on your way to your Life Purpose. People, places, and things start falling into place.

Your Preparation Stages

These beginning chapters are your preparation stages, like using the best soil and regularly watering your seed until it sprouts. Without making a real mental and/or emotional shift, very little change or clarity will occur. This is a pro-active path, not a passive one, although some level of passivity is required. The Miracle-Minded always keep the proactive and the passive in balance.

This Life Purpose coaching program is for you who have not yet learned of, or are uncertain about your Life Purpose. You may have experienced some false starts like I did. Perhaps you have not yet realized your Dreams through traditional methods, but instead found frustration and disappointment. Instead of resorting to the old uninspired methods, I'll share with you how I learned of my Life Purpose and, even more surprisingly ... a Vision of the future!

Fuel for Your Soul

Learn of your Life Purpose through what the Miracle-Minded think of as your inner wisdom, higher Self, or Higher Power. The Miracle-Minded know that when you obtain Spiritual richness in your inner life first, it fuels your outer life to be equally rich. It does so by acting upon your experience so it can become everything that brings you joy. In other words, your Spiritual awareness is the fuel that moves you forward in your life.

You've heard the saying, *"Happiness and fulfillment is an inside job!"* You'll learn how the metaphysically minded (those who explore the deeper questions of existence and reality) go about activating happiness and fulfillment in their careers and lives.

I'll get right to the point. The metaphysically minded make a distinct and purposeful connection with their higher Self and their Higher Power. I like to use the term Higher Power and/or Spirit, and you can interchange those two words for the words Spirit/God or any God of your heart. It doesn't matter what words you use as long as they're meaningful to you.

The goal is to tap into your Higher Power's vibration, wisdom, love, and guidance because you are a part of it and it's a part of you. Spiritual wisdom is a real super power and it's always available to you. Some people easily tap into their Divine inner Voice and others struggle with hearing anything, yet still rely on the more subtle intuition. This coaching program will help you with hearing your inner guidance and taking appropriate action. Both are key to Learning Your Life Purpose!

I'll share my unique stories of how I tapped into this sacred connection at the tender age of five and developed it further throughout the years through consistent study and practice. I'll share how you can do that too but in an easier and quicker way. We are all a part of the One Universal Mind so it's completely natural. Any effort to develop your awareness of your Spiritual life has immense benefits such as learning your Life Purpose.

Train for Self-Empowerment

Sure, you might be able to empower yourself by using the Law of Attraction, which for many people is hit or miss. Some people are successful and many give up after a while, frustrated by not attracting their desired material objects. This teaching is not specifically about acquiring material objects, although the gifts meant for you arrive naturally in their own time. True self-empowerment is about learning the techniques and using the tools that help you acquire a happier future and what you are here to Divinely accomplish. It's yours and it's waiting for you!

The Spiritual book, *A Course in Miracles,* talks about the Storehouse where everything that belongs to you is waiting there for you. No one can take it from you or stop you. What's stored there ... the gifts of Spirit and more are yours.

This program is about something much more powerful than materialism. It's about reprogramming your mind to achieve your Higher Power's will for you ... to serve the world in a way that is win-win-win for your Higher Power, you, and those who need your gifts and light.

My goal is to help you navigate the New Frontier by building a Spiritual foundation that connects and aligns you with your higher Self and your Higher Power. As a Co-Creator it's easier, more natural, more inspiring, and more fun than you might imagine and ... imagination is everything!

Put Your Passion Into Perspective

Like myself, you'll discover definite advantages to developing your spiritual awareness and hearing strong inner guidance! You've read from my personal story that passion was not the reason I signed up for graphic design classes. Yet there was a strong passionate outcome due to the wisdom of my inner guidance, who knew what was best for me.

Regarding your life work ... you might have a Dream or fantasy that you feel you should pursue. If so, what are you waiting for? Or maybe you have no ideas? In a way, that's good. It allows you to be open-minded when it comes to exploring your options. You'll investigate your many preferences and options in an upcoming chapter.

Not knowing what you want might leave you feeling lost and confused as to your life direction. And that's what you're looking for right now ... your best life direction. Please be patient, have faith that the answer is within you, and keep asking and exploring until you learn the way.

Label Your Life Journey

There are many labels for defining your Life Purpose or lifelong Dreams. You may desire to Live Your Dream, Go on a Mission, Follow Your Passion, or Create Life Goals. These ideas and their definitions are generally interchangeable and on some level the same, yet with slight differences. I've chosen to incorporate all of these labels into one so I avoid repetition and confusion. From now on I will refer to your *"Ideal Life Path"* instead of bouncing around with labels. I use it as an umbrella term for, *"follow your Dream, your Mission, your Calling, your Vision, your Life Purpose* or any other names for similar goals." It covers everything you can imagine without restrictions or confusion.

I believe everyone is on purpose and there are a number of purposes you'll fulfill throughout your life: mother, wife, parent, homemaker, career position, etc. Your Ideal Life Path is the one most suitable for what you're meant to do in the present moment.

There's no doubt these important aspirations ... they all lead to a higher ideal of yourself and the path that brings your imaginary desires to fruition. You may still want to privately put a label on your Ideal Life Path so that you'll know how to talk to yourself and others about your specific desires. Even though they are very similar, there are subtle differences in their execution.

I've experienced these labels throughout my life and you'll learn a few examples of how they came to my awareness and played out for me. They may remind you of similar experiences that you've had.

Labels for your Ideal Life Path

Here's a brief and simple explanation of interchangeable labels for your Ideal Life Path:

Live Your Dream—You've made up a Dream with a capital "D" of an idealized life for yourself. You see yourself attaining high levels of success. Many Dreams are of grandeur or humanitarian efforts. You may or may not be passionate about them.

Your BIG Dream—This BIG Dream is a task given you by Spirit during your sleep or meditation practice. It's a gift you give to everyone, not just yourself.

Vision—Your Vision is a Big Idea of something you'll want to accomplish. Perhaps Spirit has given you an assignment? A Vision might also come to you in a nighttime dream or meditative state. Take it seriously if it's clear/succinct.

A Mission—A Mission is determined by how strongly you feel toward some outcome in your life or in the life of a company or non-profit entity. It's what you're committed to doing to make a difference in the world.

Life Goals—These goals are the ultimate manifestations of physical experiences you want to achieve: buy a home, have children, travel to exotic locations, start a business, or follow a particular career path to its crest.

Your Passion—Your passion is your strong emotional connection. You have a need to explore your past and present to reveal a career or hobby that brings you joy, satisfaction, prosperity, and growth.

Learn Your Life Purpose—What I am here to help you with! Keep reading.

Your Gift—A special skill or talent that you possess. It's something that you are really good at doing: public speaking, singing, playing a musical instrument, an athletic sport, cooking, psychic awareness etc.

Your Calling—This could be a special talent or something you're passionate about: a certain business or to live/work in a particular location. You may feel called to serve in the military, save the environment, excavate for ancient artifacts, or help preserve Native American Tribal lands.

A Tool for Your Personal Growth

Read this brief explanation below of various life paths. Which one can you identify with?

Are YOU on a Mission!

Do you feel strongly about a certain organization; their goals and values, worldview, and the results they've achieved? If so, you might be on a mission to help make a difference in the world. You might find a purposeful life with an organization whose values align with yours.

You may have strong feelings and a personal mission to start your own non-profit organization and run it according to your own insight, meaning, and purpose. Your innovative ideas, community connections, financial resources, and inspiration could be cornerstones to make a difference in your community.

***A Mission**—*Bay Area Community Resources* is a non-profit that builds healthy communities. I worked in the tobacco education program and felt strongly aligned with their mission to help individuals, groups, and émigré's quit using tobacco products. I made it my mission too. Associating with this San Francisco non-profit gave meaning and purpose to my life.*

Answer Your Calling!

Many people feel called to a certain profession, to live in a certain location or to apply themselves to a particular cause. When it comes to your calling, you may have a feeling in your body, or feel an emotion, or you may actually hear an inner Voice that calls to you. But don't rule out the possibility that a stranger or even someone you know could be the conduit for you hearing and answering your call.

You'll read from the two following stories that a calling is also a spiritual experience leading to an Ideal Life Path. There might be a situation or experience that you dreamt or fantasized about over the years. It may or may not be something you actually intended to do. People fantasize about all kinds of experiences and never get around to doing them. On the other hand, Spirit steps in and gives you that gift. Here are three stories of how a simple calling led to big life changes.

*** **A Surprise Gift**—I drove to Baja Mexico to revisit a popular resort area. My intention was to stay about two months until I would be accepted for an apartment near where I formerly lived in Northern California.

Within a week of arriving there I twice experienced a surprising literal verbal calling of my first name. I didn't actually acknowledge it as anything important until later in the week when I shared this experience with friends.

I explained that over the years I had visited several expat communities in Mexico, but none had really "called to me." For me, Mexico always felt like home and my intention was to retire in a warm climate with a more moderate cost of living. In that moment of sharing, I surprised myself when I realized I had been called and my Dream of living in Mexico was in alignment with my Higher Power. I felt satisfied to live in this beautiful and vibrant resort area. I enjoyed ten months of living in Mexico before my guidance was to return to California. I was confused about the return, but still followed my Guidance.*

*** **Hindsight Can be Insight!**—Only in hindsight did I realize the main reason why my inner Guide said to me, *"It's time to go home."* I felt it was because of this new book and the online meditation course I was working on. The U.S. would likely be a better place to promote my book and workshops.

Six months after returning to California with a new health insurance plan and a new doctor, we discovered I had melanoma, a serious and sometimes deadly form of skin cancer. A quick biopsy and surgery removed the large tumor before it spread. That guidance, along with listening and complying, saved my life … and listening could save yours. *

*** **Inner Hearing**—Deirdra is a young woman who owned a small business in the Mexican resort town where I lived. We became fast friends, as she was friendly, welcoming, and always eager to offer her support. She told me this brief story after I told her of my personal experiences with hearing an inner Voice. I suspected that she revealed this information only because I was forthcoming about my ability to hear an inner Voice.

Shortly after she arrived in this town, she heard an inner Voice that said, *"She would live there for a very long time."* Fortunately, she appeared to enjoy her life there. She found happiness and many expat friends, along with a successful business.*

You Might be Clairaudient

I've taken this passage from my new book, *"The Art of Listening to Your Heart and Soul: Awaken to Your Intuition and Inner Guidance."*

"Clairaudience is all about hearing stuff that isn't coming from the usual sources. It may be like someone is talking to you when nobody's around or hearing music playing when there's no radio on. It's about getting messages from the Spirit world through your ears instead of visual i.e. your eyes. Individuals who are clairaudient might hear voices, sounds, or even music that others don't. I believe that most, if not all, people are clairaudient on some level, especially if they're actively creating some variation of art." It's a gift from Spirit, given to all!

You either learned to listen to your intuition (inner learning) or trained yourself to hear an inner Voice through your metaphysical studies. Here are some examples from a person who is clairaudient: You might have a significant dream that leads you in a different direction. A solution might be mentioned in a conversation and it rings true for you. A light goes on in your head bringing you a new and revealing idea. You may have an experience in a class that calls you to a certain occupation. I suggest you not dismiss the words you hear when no one is around. It's most likely your Higher Power.

Your Next Steps

In "Chapter One" you've explored some of the advantages of the Spiritual path, and how it's your Higher Power that'll lead you to your Ideal Life Path. To discover and align with your Life Purpose, start by seeking clarity and understanding the areas of life causing you pain or dissatisfaction.

Embrace a mindset shift by keeping an open mind and listening to your higher guidance, moving away from fear-based thinking. Label your Ideal Life Path by exploring various personal experiences such as dreams, visions, missions, life goals, and callings. Continuously connect with your inner wisdom and Higher Power to navigate your journey, making empowered decisions that bring joy and purpose to your life.

Now it's time to question everything: every thought, desire, or motivation. "Chapter Two" will help you clarify the meaningful from the meaningless.

CHAPTER TWO

QUESTION EVERYTHING!

There are the seven critical questions you may be asking yourself as you enter this new phase of your life. Who are you? What are you here to do, be, or learn...and when do you do it? I'll firstly answer these questions (according to what I've learned), and you should also be answering them according to your own first-hand experiences. The first most important question that many people need to ask themselves is, *"Why do I want to learn my purpose on Earth?"*

You're not here to aimlessly roam the streets but to find happiness and meaning in your life experiences and perhaps contribute to a better life and world for yourself and others. My purpose is to assist you in your metaphysical understanding of your past, present, and future life. As a Spiritual Midwife my intent is to help you birth the life your Higher Power intends for you ... the purpose you came here to achieve. I personally believe that you and I are on a Spiritual Adventure! Believe it or not, the Spiritual Adventure is designed to inspire and delight you ... if you allow it!

When you allow the adventure and remove the blocks or boulders to a Spiritual presence in your life it will shift from a hellish experience to more of a heavenly one. That's the idea or goal! Ask anyone who's achieved his/her Ideal Life Path. Every detail may or may not be perfect or easy, but that person has found an element of happiness, and more. They've found their "why?"

You might think the Universe takes fiendish pleasure in playing, 'seek and do not fine with your destiny.' The Universe will give you the answers to these questions when it feels it's important for you to know. Until then, you're knowingly or unknowingly preparing yourself for it. Once you awaken to it, you'll learn from my various stories and the chapter, "The Changing Path," that things move very quickly.

Seven Critical Life Questions

For the Miracle-Minded, these personal questions are usually answered through inner exploration ... meditation, guided imagery, or your dreams. For a quick start, here are the Miracle-Minded answers I discovered. I would like to share them with you. Make a note of your own answers as you read on.

Critical Question #1: What is Your Life Purpose or Ideal Life Path?

This is the number one question that most everyone concerns themselves with at some point in their lives: what is my life purpose? Since you have only one life here as the person you are, you want to make the most of your relatively brief time here on Earth. Eckhart Tolle, the Spiritual teacher and bestselling author says we have two purposes. One is an inner purpose and the other is an outer purpose.

The Miracle-Minded believe your inner purpose is one that encompasses everyone. Your inner purpose is to awaken to your true Spiritual identity as a *'Spiritual being living in the experience of a physical body.'* You may think the more important part is the 'physical body experience,' but it's the other way around. Who you are in truth, a Spiritual being, is an image created by Light and Love. You are a Being who is expected to "BE who you are ... a beloved Spirit," not your controlling ego. And also accept that your crotchety neighbor, your defiant cousin, your complaining aunt, and your demanding boss have the same Spiritual identity. Yeah, that's the tough part! Don't give up hope, as I'll address this challenge in a future chapter.

You'll also discover, learn, or awaken to your outer purpose. It's often thought to be your ultimate passion and/or contribution to our humanity. It may also have something to do with your karma or personal accountability. Your outer purpose or Ideal Life Path may be revealed through your intuition, imagination, dreams, meditation state, chanting, or through other methods, but it's always in connection with your Higher Power.

These answers allude to what the ancients have been telling us for eons ... that we are actually asleep, dreamers dreaming a dream of separation, sadness, suffering, and death. Awaken to your Spiritual reality and that dream ends. The Dream of happiness and peace begins. * What do YOU think is your Life Purpose/Ideal Life Path?

Critical Question #2: Who Are You?

To the Miracle-Minded, who you are is not who you see in a mirror ... a bodily image that may be temporarily lost, confused, and in pain. As a Spirit having a human experience, you have an absolute Spiritual connection to your Higher Power, to every other person, and every thing (dogs, bears, birds, nature etc.) that has a Spirit. You may call that Oneness!

That powerful truth allows you to perceive yourself and everyone else differently. You now have a new and different Identity! It's holy, sacred, spiritual, and Spirit-empowered. Listen up, because this is a BIG DEAL!

You'll learn and remember to shift your Identity from body-focused to Spirit-focused. You'll shift your mindset because you're no longer the same person filled with fear and separated from your Higher Power. You're Spirit! You're free of the limitations of your ego! You're connected to your Source! Your reality changes in either subtle or not-so-subtle ways. All of these realities eventually align with who you really are once your mind accepts the truth of who you are. You may experience radical changes in your thoughts and perceptions leading you to become more Spiritually oriented.

It matters less what people look like on the outside: skin, eye, hair color, or physical appearance. Their body is not who they are. It's about their Spiritual presence, how they shine their light, and how they show up in the world that makes a statement and a real difference.

Socrates, the ancient Greek philosopher claimed that the unexamined life is not worth living. He said, *"Know thyself"* and *"To know thyself is the beginning of wisdom."* Knowing yourself is like having a compass to direct your path. Socrates also said, *"The only true wisdom is in knowing you know nothing."* This is a very humbling statement. By admitting you know nothing are you able to learn anew through honest self-examination and through your relationship experiences. * Who do YOU think you are?

Critical Question #3: What Are You Here to Do?

Metaphysically speaking, you're here to do things that only you can do or do your thing in a way that is unique to you. You are here to utilize your special talents or gifts, be who you are, and do it in a way that brings joy to yourself and others! You may not become a big movie star, but you can still be a hero/heroine! Perhaps you don't think you're here to make a big splash. Not everyone can be President of the United States, run a top corporation, become a famous actor or actress, or a world-class athlete. Not everyone has the ambition to achieve a high performance lifestyle. That doesn't mean you can't do good things or be a hero to yourself, your family, or your community.

You might be the type of hero or heroine who is here to give of yourself, support others, or give birth to someone who changes the world. It might not be about you struggling to become a CEO but about giving birth to and raising a child or children who affect the world in positive ways.

In fact, what you're doing is giving birth on a regular basis. It may be the birth of a new way of thinking or perceiving, or the birth of a business, college degree, or a new adventure. Birthing desires or actions are what you, as a human, are destined to do. Hopefully you'll birth a more kind, loving, and joyful world. That's what this coaching program is about.

Did the mothers of Albert Einstein, Elon Musk, or Bill Gates know they were going to birth and raise a genius? Probably not! It's possible to know the answer, as their mothers are Spiritually connected too.

Biblical stories tell us that an Angel visited Jesus' mother, Mary, when she was a teenager. The Angel told her she would bring a Savior into the world and the father would be God, not her husband Joseph.

On one hand, to modern society, that may sound like a fairly radical prediction. On the other hand, Christians and the Miracle-Minded also believe the One God is the Father to us all ("Our Father who art in Heaven" ...). It turns out not to be such a radical prediction, doesn't it?

By the same token, many men and women may be considered saviors. Perhaps not in the same vein as Jesus, who also revealed the Christ Consciousness that we may aspire to, but through their selfless acts of heroism or healing. Think 9/11, worldwide climate-related fires, the 2020 Covid-19 pandemic, and other natural disasters. First responders and regular people rise to the occasion to save the day for those in peril. In my mind, they are saviors too!

What are you here to do? You're here to serve the world in some capacity that you'll explore throughout this program. You'll look within - LITERALLY - to reveal your specific Dream or learn of your Ideal Life Path. It's waiting there for you to discover ... like it was for me. These first few chapters will prepare you for that revelation. * What do YOU think you're here to do?

Critical Question #4: Who Are You Here to Be?

You're here to play various parts or roles like an actor or actress. You'll discover those parts as you interact with others or delve more deeply inside yourself. Most importantly, you're here to be a light to the world, to extend love and offer forgiveness wherever it's needed.

Can you achieve a low profile, high happiness life? There are many people who are completely satisfied with a quiet, low profile life. They have Dreams too, but at a more relaxed level than some of us. They still make a comfortable living, explore the world, express themselves through art or hobbies, enjoy their family and friends, and that's enough for them!

*** **Enjoy Your Life**—My longtime friends, Jim and Trudi, are two such people. They lead a happy and comfortable life. Jim made his fortune in real estate, but also enjoys auto racing as a hobby. Trudi was a top hair stylist in the town where they live. She also raced cars, won awards like her husband, and now finds great pleasure in playing the game of bridge with friends. They're both fulfilled and enjoy their lives.* Who are YOU here to be?

Critical Question #5: What Are You Here to Learn?

You'll learn wisdom lessons through your interactions with other people or any desired endeavors. You'll learn a lot about yourself (your strengths and weaknesses) as you step into various situations: romantic relationships, co-working relationships, starting a business, raising children, or otherwise making your way in the world.

Life will challenge you on many fronts until you review and answer these seven questions. While your Spirit is essentially perfect, your human experience doesn't always reflect that truth. Your ego may have a different agenda and may be hiding your truth. Your highest goal, with the help of Spirit, is to bring that perfection to your daily life.

You might be asking, *"Why haven't I learned of my Ideal Life Path if it's so important?"* Some people do learn their Ideal Life Path at an early age, mostly due to the long, necessary training period. Think Tiger Woods or other world-class athletes, musicians, or artists who begin their training in childhood. It takes many years to become a world-class athlete or professional artist. They often accomplish their Big Dream earlier in life, and later search for their second act.

The solution here is to be patient! There may be many more things you need to learn or experience to be in the best position for your Dreams to manifest.* What are YOU here to Learn?

*** **The Wiser Way**—I didn't learn my life purpose until I was middle aged. I ended my former career due to burn out. Then I had to do a fair amount of mental exploration and academic research. That meant looking at career options and narrowing down my choices until I was ready to make an important decision for my happiness. You'll do the same in the chapter, The Process of Discovery. Spirit allowed me my choices and decisions, but still led me along the *wiser way* that I didn't know existed. As I followed, I was grateful to receive clarity mainly through my intuition, dreams, and other guidance that I'll reveal to you.*

What are YOU here to learn? Will you follow *your wiser way*?

Critical Question #6: Why Do You Want to Know and Obtain Your Ideal Life Path?

Think about "why" you want to know and obtain your Ideal Life Path? Is there something personal you want to accomplish? Why is that? Do you want to make the world a better place? Why is that? Do you want to have a better life for yourself and your family? Why is that? When you find an answer, keep asking yourself *why* you want that and go deeper until you get to your truth. It's because your truth will lead you to your Ideal Life Path. Your truth is your fast lane, so answer the questions and steer into it. Knowing your "why" helps with focus, motivation, and decision making.

* Know your "why" and the "how" happens naturally. What is YOUR "Why?"

Critical Question #7: When and Where Do You Start?

This is an easy question to answer. Now that you know "why" you're interested in learning your Ideal Life Path, you can start right here, right now, right where you are! Put your unhappiness in the past where it belongs and take steps to make sure it stays that way. You'll do that in upcoming chapters. The Miracle-Minded review the past then leave it behind. Take the love and life lessons into the future, allowing it to support you through any challenges you encounter.* When and where will YOU start?

Your Next Steps

This second chapter is an intention to help you answer these critical questions, give you clarity, and encourage you to take the necessary steps toward following that still small Voice within.

Reflect on the seven critical questions and align them with any Dreams you may be courting. Consider your true Identity as a Spiritual being and identify what unique contributions you might be here to make and/or the roles you are meant to play.

Recognize the wisdom you're meant to learn from your life's challenges. What has been your experience so far? Clarify your motivations for seeking your Ideal Life Path by deeply exploring your "why." Finally, commit to starting this journey now, letting go of past unhappiness and embracing a future guided by love and Spiritual insight.

Compare my answers to these seven questions with your own. Does anything jump out at you or did you read anything that inspired you? After reviewing your answers, let's move on because your Ideal Life Path is patiently waiting for your arrival.

CHAPTER THREE
IT'S TIME TO COURSE-CORRECT

Let's move on from your primary Spiritual questions and answers to focus on some fundamental situations, insights and solutions. Now is the time to explore your next steps in the amazing future that is meant for you. As you've read in "Chapter One," the odds are that you're not just a statistic, but are left in the doldrums over your past career or relationship disappointments. That has to be dealt with or it's likely to repeat itself. You don't want that. It's best to shift forward, review any errors and correct them so you're free of them once and for all. No errors? You might question that perception too. Let's learn how to shift mindfully to course-correct.

For example, you can model what professional racecar drivers do to correct their errors and improve their performance. They videotape themselves to review their prior performance, especially if it was less than stellar. As they review their dismal performance, they get insight and learn how to correct their actions for the next time. They essentially relearn how to strategically maneuver the track or course, their racecar, and their mindset in a more impactful way.

Obviously, recording your past work or relationship performance is impossible, but if you've developed some level of self-awareness, you most likely know what errors caused a problem. It's often mindset or attitudinal, so you'll look at that to learn if it's something that can be changed so the error doesn't happen again. Just know that the process of reviewing and correcting errors benefits you. You're correcting misperceptions that could hold you back from your future Ideal Life Path or relationships. To Course-correct is about transforming emotional pain into wisdom and healing.

*** Learn to Shift Gears—My younger brother, Bill, bought a cool classic convertible after he graduated from college. I knew I wanted to drive it but it was a stick shift and my experience was driving an automatic transmission. One day he asked me if I wanted to drive his car? He was kind enough to teach me how to do it. I first had to shift my mindset to a different way of driving. I had to learn how to coordinate my right hand with the stick and adjust my feet on the pedals. It took a little while for me to get the process. Fortunately, Bill was patient through my rocky starts and stops until I learned to shift the gears into a smooth transition.

Personal transformation is much like learning to shift gears—not a stick shift but a mind shift. There will be rocky starts and stops until you get to a smooth transition. You'll be learning new habits, techniques, and processes, just like I did with my brother's convertible. When your work or life appears to be stuck in one gear, to get moving again is to shift into a new mindset and a gear that moves you forward. Doing so improves your situation, the one after that, and the next one. *

A Tool for Personal Growth

Transform Emotional Stress Into Wisdom —A Body Scan & Guided Imagery

You're going to start with a brief Body Scan to allow your body/mind to relax. This relaxation process will help you let go of any discomfort or stress you're holding. You'll release it to be in the present moment for a necessary personal journey into your past. The goal here is to step back in time, mentally and Spiritually, to a time when you had a grievance with a co-worker or former relationship. Just like the previous example of a racecar driver, you're learning to course-correct.

Body Scan: Read this body scan process first before you begin.

(Start with your head and work your way down to your toes if you are using this visualization for journeying. Start at your toes and work up to your head if your visualization is about using your mind to achieve a specific goal.)

Close your eyes. Take a few deep breaths. Breathe in, hold, let go, and take two more deep breaths. Relax your muscles from your feet to the top of your head. Name each body part as you ask it to relax. (Example: *"I feel all the muscles in my toes and feet begin to unwind and relax." "I move that relaxed and comfortable feeling up into the calf muscles, knees, and thighs."*) Continue naming muscles all the way to the top of your head. Take your time.

"Like loose rubber bands, I allow all the muscles in my stomach, abdomen, chest, back, fingers, hands, arms, shoulders, neck, and face to completely relax."

As you become more relaxed and comfortable, you find yourself in a peaceful place, perhaps a beautiful garden or serene beach where you feel safe and secure. Look around in your imagination and acknowledge the scene that brings you comfort. Continue to feel safe and encircled by a beautiful, soft golden light that helps you also feel warm and nurtured. As you continue to gaze into your peaceful environment, you notice someone you know or used to know. This person who you may have felt animosity towards is also engulfed with a sacred and golden light ... just like you. That individual sits next to you on a bench and smiles warmly at you. You smile in return and begin a kind and thoughtful dialogue about your past relationship. You both have questions and answers. Spend a few minutes each reviewing former situations and possible errors. Continue your dialogue until you get clarity and come to a peaceful understanding that you are both satisfied with.

Allow the part of you that was unhappy to make a shift into a new and better perception and mindset. Thank that person for joining you. When you're ready, come back into the room. Stretch your body and take a few minutes to review your experience. What insight did you receive? How did that change you?

Build a Better Mindset

Learning how to move on from setbacks is a matter of willingness. At some point you'll face a setback or two on your journey to your Ideal Life Path. Setbacks are natural and learning how to deal with errors or failures makes you a stronger and more resilient person. When your Higher Power comes knocking on your door, you'll be ready to tackle anything.

Three Helpful Ways to Build a Better Mindset

Let go of what doesn't work and move on to the mindset that supports you.

1. Shift Your Mindset: When you are stuck with doldrums and disappointments, it's time to shift from a mindset that no longer serves you and move on to one that does. All things change in this world and flowing with the changes must be seen as an opportunity and not a loss. Shift your attitude so you see possibilities and opportunities in front of you, not a life of struggle, pain, and suffering. When you aren't able to manifest the things or experiences you dream or fantasize about, I suggest you either try a better tactic or just play it straight. Let it go and move on to something else that has potential. That's what I did. In the times where I didn't see a path forward, I didn't waste time, I shifted and took another attractive path and eventually got back on course.

2. Do a Reframe: Use your brain to mentally re-frame your losses, disappointments, or failures in a way that still allows you to retain your dignity. You may not win the competition, the award, or the VIP role. Instead, you can choose to win back your confidence, tenacity, and motivation because you were bold enough to take on a risk. A lot can be said for that.

There's a gift in any positive or negative situation whether you deem the results of that situation as successful or not. It's there if you are open minded enough to see it and receive it. Give yourself credit for all actions taken, full or partial wins, your resiliency, and any positive outcomes. How can you reframe a disappointing situation, take away an important lesson, and still feel good about yourself for doing your best?

3. Find Your Takeaways: Experience is the best teacher. The real value lies in what you learned that's a takeaway for future experiences. Determine what you learned from an unfortunate experience, pick yourself up, and start over. You'll take on the next risk and the next, to discover the many rewards the Universe offers you for your intentions and efforts. Apply everything you learned to your next experience to make it better or more successful.

SUCCESS SKILLS

The necessary skill for a successful rebirth and a new and better life is a *positive mindset*. Let it be okay that every situation doesn't always turn out the way you think it should. Know there are better places for you to shine your light. There's a Divine plan for your life and that undesirable situation is either a stepping-stone to it or just not a fit. Let it go and move on.

A Tool for Your Personal Growth

What upsetting situation in your life could be reframed in a way that brings you to a point of peace and understanding? Choose at least one situation where you could turn it around and use it to support your next adventure. Start with the Body Scan and transform a less than stellar situation into one that delights you.

*** **Be Perceptive!**—It was 2009 and the economy started a downturn. I observed the establishment where I worked for just six months make major unannounced changes: they painted the inside and outside of the building, cleaned out the storage area, and quit advertising. Within a month or so they sold the building and we were quietly laid off. There was no formal notice, but I watched the changes happening and expected the layoff. The media finally labeled that period of time "The Great Recession." Allow your perceptions to see the truth around you.*

Shift Forward by Identifying Triggers

Do you dislike your current career, job, or the people you work with? Does your frustration and fear keep you in a constant loop of disappointment and inaction? It's time to move forward by identifying the triggers that hold you back and prevent you from taking action towards learning your Ideal Life Path. Do a reality check by visiting these four triggers that may be holding you back!

Trigger #1: Red flags are not an accident. Acknowledge them! They're designed to shake you up to wake you up! Frustration, fear, misery, and pain are red flags and signals that you've lost your way, passion, or enthusiasm and it could be time for a change.

Trigger #2: Pay attention to what's going on around you. Notice different or suspicious behaviors or attitudes at your workplace. There are often subtle signs that change is coming your way, as when my former employer refreshed her building.

Trigger #3: Has a light turned on in your head? Does something click for you that your joy has gone? Be mindful of your feelings and do something about them before they become destructive actions.

Trigger #4: Pay attention to your emotions. They are a critical body-related trigger telling you to either move in one direction or another. You'll read from Daniela's personal story that these experiences of frustration and discomfort are triggers eventually leading to a better life experience. That's why it's best not to fight it but analyze it and follow your heart.

Let's take a look at how this idea played out for a young woman named Daniela, and what you can learn from her experience.

*** Click—Daniela is a young woman who knew her calling, but required a better opportunity. She is an intelligent, attractive, and vibrant young lady who appeared, on the outside, to find happiness with her sales position at a retail and wholesale wine company. She had good things to say about her experience.

I was surprised when Daniela later revealed she quit her job. She planned to move to another wine-focused location to pursue her love of the industry. Since I hadn't spoken with her for a while, she disclosed that she still loved the wine-related profession, but experienced a shift in her happiness with her current employer. She wasn't paid the money she was under contract for and felt underappreciated for all the long hours she put into her work.

She said one day it just clicked for her, as I watched her snap her fingers, and Daniela knew she would have to leave. Her epiphany came to her once she reassessed her growing displeasure for being treated unfairly. Her desire for a city experience and a different wine/food-focused location drew her curiosity, passion, and sense of adventure. Daniela moved on to a better situation where she could follow her Ideal Life Path and find a better working relationship.*

Tools for Your Personal Growth

Ask yourself important questions:

1. What do you think stops you, zaps your inner strength, and holds you back from the life you want?

2. No worries! Was there ever a time in your life when you worried about an outcome and your worries turned out to be unwarranted?

3. Was there a time you trusted in the Universe and it served you better!

The Five Roadblocks Holding You Back

There are five roadblocks that may be holding you back from learning your purpose! Where does the confusion come from?

Roadblock #1: You might have too many options from which to choose!

Solution: Narrow your options. Choose only the options that bring you joy ... no more than three!

Roadblock #2: You may not be focusing on ways to get clarity from your intuition!

Solution: Remember to listen for repetition and subtle inner messages from your inner Voice or higher Self. Pay attention to your feelings/emotions.

Roadblock #3: Were you following someone else's lead and not your own heart? Your heart speaks of your truth. Listen to it in all situations.

Solution: Start over and follow your own heart. The previous tool will help you.

Roadblock #4: You may not have a strong Spiritual connection to guide you!

Solution: My Goal-Directed Meditation program can help you align with your Spirit-inspired goals.

Roadblock #5: You looked outside yourself!

Solution: Currently, many people are directed toward technology careers. It's right for some people, but not everyone ... depending on your career needs. Look at it and then decide if it's a path that feeds your soul.

Remember: You have all the answers within you. What roadblocks and solutions may apply to your situation? Write them here:

Your Next Steps

After reading "Chapter Three: Shift Mindfully to Course Correct," reflect on past mistakes in your career or relationships. Use your self-awareness to identify areas for improvement. Practice a mindset shift by making small, positive changes in your daily habits. Practice patience and listening intently.

Regularly perform guided imagery sessions to release stress and gain insights. Embrace setbacks as learning opportunities, reframe negative experiences positively and focus on the lessons they offer. Pay attention to emotional triggers that point out the need for change and proactively address them. And finally, implement some of the included strategies to overcome any obstacles, and align yourself with your Spirit-inspired and personal goals.

CHAPTER FOUR

BECOME MIRACLE-MINDED!

An important step to learning about and achieving your Ideal Life Path is to become Miracle-Minded. Why is that? The Miracle-Minded know that having a simple *shift in one's outlook* can change any fearful thoughts about what is meant for you. You may fear never learning about, not liking, or not being able to accomplish your purpose in life. It's nonsensical to think your Higher Power, your Divine Father, would do that to a child He loves. Your Higher Power knows you intimately and acts in your best interests. You can trust that both miracles and a perfectly created purpose are either already manifesting for you or on its way to you.

ACIM relates, more or less, that a shift in perception from fear to love is a miracle. It's a miracle because you and I know it's not always simple or easy to change your mind when you're in fear or despair. You tend to stay in fear unless you're given a strong reason to shift away from it. Or you may be able to pull strength from deep within you to overcome the fear (despair, anger, negativity, jealousy, control). That Divine strength from deep within is your Higher Power's strength, not your meager human strength. You may need that extra *edge* to get to the place your Higher Power wills for you. The primary thing that's asked of you … is to go to your Higher Power first for guidance and tap into His strength in order to drop the fear!

You've been taught to think of a miracle as a highly unusual situation that rarely ever happens, such as a mother lifting a car from her son who is trapped underneath. That is truly a Divine miracle of love, support, and strength. This new interpretation of a miracle allows you to use it in your daily life, and you know that life sometimes requires a daily Miracle-Mind.

*** Get Over It—A small group of us children around the ages of 10 or so spent the day at Riverview Park, a large amusement park outside of Chicago. I rode all the amusement rides with my friends except for the roller coasters. A prior frightening experience kept me from joining them. Since they spent most of the day riding the coasters, I spent most of my day standing by the sidelines watching them. I distinctly remember thinking, near the end of the day, that I must be missing out on something. In a moment it occurred to me that maybe, just maybe it wouldn't be so bad. I built up my inner strength and followed my friends up the platform. I had the time of my life ... and never looked back, both literally and figuratively. It's still my favorite ride in the park.*

You may have had fearful thoughts in the past, so you know how fear stops you from advancing. Your Higher Power wants only for your happiness, so you're going against that vision for you by holding thoughts of fear, despair, or grievances.

Fearful thoughts may also hold you back from confronting someone who has harmed you in some way, leaving you with feelings of anxiety or worthlessness. When you mindfully confront someone who spoke out against you—you correct the balance in the relationship, build self-confidence, and earn self-respect. Instead of becoming a doormat—be the doorway to a healthy relationship.

Instead of wallowing in fear over seemingly difficult decisions, shifting to a miraculous loving thought allows you to step up and stoke your confidence to take that much needed vacation, forgive your parents, or start that side hustle. You'll never know what will come of it if you don't loose the fear. If you feel guided to shift into freedom, then just do it!

*** Open for Business—Overcoming fearful thoughts opens the way to a new life experience. It was during my mid twenties when I experienced frustration ... not with my career choice, but with my employer. I became tired of the constant intimidation. My work was excellent, yet this person constantly picked at me causing tears and anger.

I often fantasized about becoming self-employed. It was the mid 1970's and I didn't have much money, the economy was in a downturn, and there were many similar businesses in my small hometown. Those limiting beliefs caused me to become skeptical towards my Dream of self-employment. I almost gave up and changed professions but my guidance was to continue, follow my heart, and stay in a fun and creative field.

After talking with a co-worker and then getting additional clarity through my inner Guide, I decided to go ahead with my original business plans. I let go of my fear, a miracle occurred and I was ready to step up to who I was meant to be.

As we co-created a new opportunity I was led in creative ways to inexpensively buy the equipment and supplies I needed and ignore the economy

... realizing I'd be off to a slow start. Competition didn't scare me ... it drove me!

A supportive co-worker happily joined me in my new endeavor and that made all the difference. Five years later I closed that location and moved to a better location. Ah yes, success is sweet! An old adage: sometimes you have to crawl before you can walk.*

Shift Your Limiting Beliefs

Whatever Dream or Spirit-inspired goal you have, as in my examples, be aware that at some point fear may set in. The cause is, "limiting beliefs." Those pesky limiting beliefs (which are fear-related) may try to stop you in your tracks. Suddenly you'll say words to yourself like I did, *"There are already many businesses like mine,"* or *"The economy is bad,"* or *"I don't have enough money."* Limiting beliefs can and will hold you back from your Dreams if you believe in them and give them precedent over your life.

Fearful words are an insidious attempt by your ego to keep you from shining your light, to protect you from failure that isn't imminent, or to restrict your freedom of expression. Or perhaps fearful thoughts are your or someone else's misperceptions? It doesn't matter where the negativity came from, you must stop the fear and lean into a miracle.

Fearful thoughts may be patterns of thinking that need to be interrupted, corrected, or reframed. I'll help you make that shift in this chapter, and you'll build on everything you learned in Chapter Three! You're getting closer and closer to the person your Higher Power would have you be ... *a Spiritual being having a human experience ... and bringing a Spiritual slant to all that happens!*

Shift to a Limitless Life Path: Seven Steps to Freedom

You may become limitless by course correcting and only reflecting on your Spirit-inspired goals and Dreams. Take out your journal and let's get started with this *Seven Step Process to Be Free of Limitations!*

Step #1: The first step is to identify negative beliefs. Make a list of three negative beliefs that you believe hold you back from taking action on your Dreams. Ask yourself what *excuses* stop you from achieving your goals, commitments, or happiness. *"I don't have enough money," "I need more training," "I was born on the wrong side of the tracks," "I'm too short, fat, or unattractive."* Let all that go! Or at the very least take steps to overcome these self-inflicted inner barriers to your success. Find ways to earn more money, reduce your weight, or take low cost classes to gain new skills.

Step #2: The second step is to look at each fearful belief to determine if there's really any truth to it. 1) Is it a lie, 2) an exaggeration, 3) a misperception, or 4) just a touch of reality? Name each belief and its truth.

Step #3: Next to each belief write down an answer that satisfies you. What evidence is there to support those beliefs? Is it true or false and why?

Step #4: Determine if there's a payoff to having those fears? Maybe they worked for you in the past? Payoffs could be: you don't have to leave your comfort zone, make an effort, risk failure, go into fear, or ask others to help you. Write those excuses in your journal.

Step #5: How could you unravel those misperceptions and *look at each one differently?* How could your future be better if you had no negativity or fear? *"Money comes to me easily and effortlessly!" "I ask for a raise at work, take a part time job, or use a budget."*

Step #6: Your next step is to find *an alternate belief* that is more *empowering*. Re-interpret each negative belief and put it in a positive light. *"I trust the Universe to show me ways to increase my income."*

Write those words in your journal and ask yourself how you feel about your new empowering affirmations? Do they feel right? Can you find evidence that these new perceptions are correct? Was there ever a time in your past when you empowered yourself with these positive words? As a result, you overcame something you didn't think you could?

Re-affirm those thoughts, words, and feelings of success. Can you apply the energy of your past wins to your current situation? Do it now!

Step #7: Do a series of mental rehearsals. Practice those success words in front of a mirror. Own them! See yourself practicing with those words and achieving your Spirit-inspired goals.

Examples: *"I'm the right and perfect age to share my wisdom. My peers appreciate what I have to say." "My youthfulness and energy are beneficial and my experience in this field make an impression. My team appreciates my knowledge." "The audience listens to what I have to say because I have walked in their shoes, can share shortcuts I discovered, and my solutions are fast and cost effective."* Repeat as needed!

Tools for Your Personal Growth

1. What are your fears and limiting beliefs? Which fears hold you back? What new perceptions can turn that around?

2. What parts of the Seven Step Process can you use to shift your limiting beliefs?

SUCCESS SKILLS

The best skills to heal limiting beliefs is to become a Miracle Master: *be positive, be patient with yourself, and believe in your ability to succeed.* Use the "Seven Steps to Freedom" to squash those limiting beliefs and replace them with the truth about yourself: you can ask for either Spiritual or human guidance. Remember to use repetition, affirmations, and visualizations.

The key to overcoming many fears such as: the fear of flying in airplanes, the fear of snakes, the fear of heights or water, etc. is to. *"Increase exposure to anything you fear."* Repetition equals confidence!

Create A New Pattern

A pattern is a paper blueprint for an article of clothing or a physical building. When a seamstress follows a pattern, she gets the exact same results each time she makes that article of clothing. This is great for clothes, cupcakes, and widgets, but not for someone in transition.

Apply the concept of patterns to your thoughts and actions. If you keep the same thoughts or mindset and act on them you'll get the same results. If you don't like your results, change your thought pattern and/or your actions. Remember what author and speaker Mike Dooley says, *"thoughts become things."* This means you're responsible for what you think, do, and the results. That's how it comes to be that you're always manifesting something, so it's important to watch your thoughts like a hawk. Make mindful choices and decisions so you manifest what you truly want.

Adopt positive thought patterns and when a promising opportunity comes your way, and it will, you'll be ready with a mindset of confidence and courage to meet the moment

Your Next Steps

You've learned how to course-correct and that puts you into a great place to reclaim your Spiritual Identity. This puts you on your path of positivity as well as a step closer to embracing who you are in truth. To achieve your Ideal Life Path and learn your life purpose, become Miracle-Minded by shifting your perspective from fear to love. Trust your Higher Power's guidance rather than just guessing what to do next. Mindfulness can help you confront and overcome limiting beliefs, and redefine miracles as everyday positive changes.

You can cultivate your success skills through positivity, patience, and self-belief. Change your thought patterns to manifest desired outcomes and approach opportunities with confidence and courage.

CHAPTER FIVE

TAKE IT UP A NOTCH

Now that you've conquered your limiting beliefs and created new patterns of thought, you've put yourself in a position to "Take it Up a Notch" and start a shift into your new Spiritual Identity.

Enter a New Paradigm

To live an amazing new life unencumbered by the past, you'll find yourself entering a new paradigm that's an alternative path to others that probably haven't delivered for you. According to the Miracle-Minded, the world you see has all the trappings of the ego … faulty beliefs and vain hopes without enough regard for a Spiritual connection, which is the new paradigm.

The Miracle-Minded believe there are two strong Rulers in our world. One is an illusion and the other is Reality. The Miracle-Minded think of this as upside down perception. What you may perceive to be important isn't and what you perceive to be less important is actually the most important. Hang in there as I explain this idea.

The illusory Ruler, the one many of us tend to be slave to, is the ego or what I've labeled as ego-dum, as opposed to the real *Kingdom* of Your Higher Power.

The ego mind thinks it rules the world because it sees itself everywhere playing out in dramatic ways. Some people believe they need ego-centered thinking to get ahead. That's not true. Instead, that's insidious aggrandizement. Ego identification and its fear-based thought system are not who you really are. It's a false perception because it accepts fear and everything under the umbrella of fear: anger, judgment, control, despair, jealousy and all negativity as its reality and truth. The ego's unfortunate grandiosity may hold you back from perceiving the world as love-based and ruled by your Higher Power/God. It resists the truth that the real nature of the Universe is love and only love.

The ego doesn't have faith or trust that a Higher Power is in charge. Therefore attack thoughts toward anyone are a mistake. To do your best is all that's asked of you ... to keep trying. Here's the icing on the cake ... you are always loved by your Higher Power/Spirit ... no matter what! And that's even when you slip up, slack off, or muck it up! Other people may not like it, but your Higher Power doesn't keep score on your human faults and foibles.

Destined for Greatness

Be yourself and believe in yourself! There's no doubt that some people, and you may be one, who is destined for greatness. You may be grounded in the belief that life has more for you. I remember Oprah Winfrey, the talk show hostess, actress, businesswoman, and writer confess that she always knew she was destined for greatness.

Not everyone has a destiny like Oprah Winfrey, nor does everyone want that. Can you become a leader in your field? It could be sports, business, financials, sales, or politics. You may learn that excelling and becoming the best in your field allows you to have the appearance of greatness. Remember that greatness also has its pro's and cons.

You often hear stories about people who receive Academy Awards, Emmy's, Tony Awards, and many other trophies and accolades. They confess to the audience about 'watching television for many years and seeing other people get awards.' They had Dreams but never expected to stand on stage and receive that coveted award for themselves. Instead of limiting themselves, they believed in themselves and took the steps to make it happen.

*** **EMMY**—It's September 2022, and Sheryl Le Ralph is named Outstanding Supporting Actress in a comedy series for her role in Abbott Elementary. As she receives and holds up her Emmy award, she announces to the audience, *"To anyone who has ever had a Dream and thought their Dream couldn't, wouldn't come true, I am here to tell you this is what believing looks like ... and don't you ever, ever give up on you!"* *

New beliefs help you to take it up a notch and reach your Dreams or greatness! People of any color, gender, nationality, or age can become a leader, innovator, or talent in their field. It does happen and it could happen to you. Dream it, believe it, become it!

Secrets to Making that Shift: Happiness Now!

How do you achieve happiness now? You gain clarity, then make a purposeful shift towards its manifestation. Here's one of the secrets: *Set clear and meaningful Spirit-inspired goals that align with your values.*

Define distinct and easily achievable goals for your future version of yourself. Do you know what success looks like to you? Many people don't. I didn't. *Chapter Fifteen: Live Your Purposeful Life* can help you gain needed clarity.

*** **Busyness**—One day a customer said, *"Look Linda, at all the customers here. You're a success!"* I looked up to see that she was right. My business was booming, but my nose was to the grindstone. Darn, I almost missed it.*

Create Powerful Intentions

1) Visualize what success looks like and 2) invite it into your life ... sends a strong message to the Universe.

If your visualization is in alignment with your Higher Power's plan for your life, then you are in business! Those two intentions: the conscious act of: 1) knowing what you want and 2) asking for it sends a signal to your subconscious mind. When in alignment, your super-conscious mind brings together all the elements for it to happen or open doors for you. Your clarity and the Universe guides your thoughts and actions to make it manifest. Try this first with small desires, then your larger Dreams.

1. Positive Affirmations: You may use positive affirmations to reinforce the new image you want to create. Personal growth experts say regular affirmations can help rewire your subconscious mind, just like repetitive new actions do. It can lead you towards more empowering beliefs. Positive affirmations are always brief, start with "I Am." Affirmations are always focused in the present: *"I am peaceful, healthy, strong, and wealthy!"*- Author, Douglas Cox

2. Challenge Negative Thoughts: I personally have had more success with the results from *stopping negative thoughts in their tracks* than using positive affirmations. Don't let negative thoughts get the better of you. Stop them right away. The instant they arise in your mind, make it simple by replacing each thought with one strong word, "STOP!" Shift away from the negativity and move on. I found that my "STOP" method to be well-rewarded in about three weeks.

"Believe it and you'll see it!" – Author, Wayne Dyer.

3. Visualization: As a daily practice, visualize yourself as the *successful ideal you* that you desire to create. Visualize yourself connecting with your Higher Power and getting clear guidance. See yourself achieving your Dreams: making the connections, getting the funding, writing your business plan, and applying your marketing skills. See yourself displaying the emotions associated with the success you desire. Visualize your self as happy, peaceful, having fun, and surrounded by people who are supportive and/or loving.

4. Start a Daily Gratitude Practice: Express gratitude to the Universe or Higher Power on a daily basis. Focus on all that's good in your life and the progress you're making as you take those daily steps toward your ideal self. Express gratitude for people who are there for you and bring joy into your life. Know that gratitude multiplies itself. The more you are grateful for, the more returns to you.

5. Surround Yourself with Positive Influences: Surround yourself with influences that encourage greatness. Join a Mastermind or a Spiritual group that looks through the lens of love. Positive influences are truly good people, inspiring books, and CD's, or certain inspired television shows and movies.

You can also choose media that enriches your life. There are many free and inspiring interviews and mini-classes on YouTube. Use them, subscribe, and be grateful to Thought Leaders who contribute to uplifting humanity.

6. Limit your exposure to negativity in the news and toxic people. When I first joined FaceBook I let everyone be my friend until I realized that some people had toxic tendencies or very different values than I. Too much time spent scrolling through uninspiring dialogue and nonsensical images is wasteful of your time and energy. Now all my friends and groups are people I care about, who inspire me, and contribute to a more joyful world.

7. Take Daily Action Toward Your Goals: Break down your goals into actionable steps and start taking small, consistent actions towards your vision. Create a calendar for the month and write your intentions, marking them off once accomplished. Success breeds more success!

8. Celebrate Your Progress: Consistency is King. Determine the milestones to your Spirit-inspired goal, and acknowledge each one as it is accomplished. Celebrate through joyful feelings, high five's, and rockin' dance! Share your progress with others. Celebration reinforces the positive changes and progress you are making.

9. Mindfulness and Self-Awareness: These two practices are cornerstones of a more enlightened and happy life. The practice of mindfulness helps you become more aware of your thought patterns. When you notice negative thoughts, gently redirect your focus to the positive views you desire. Discipline is the way to create the ideal you.

10. Learn from Setbacks: Everyone experiences setbacks. Setbacks and challenges are a natural part of life and growth. Instead of being discouraged, view them as learning opportunities. See the value in adjusting your attitude! Know that something better is in store for you. When you look back at your life you'll see, in hindsight and with honest clarity, how everything worked out as planned by your Higher Power.

11. Never Take on a Victim Mentality: However your setbacks affect you, remember that any learning opportunities are there as a hidden benefit. Any diminishment you feel is temporary. The Miracle-Minded don't subscribe to being a victim! Next time you'll make a different choice or decision. You'll earn the title of Victor!

12. Surround Yourself with a Strong Support System: Share your future vision with trusted friends, mentors, or a coach. Hire a coach/mentor who can provide three critical necessities: encouragement, accountability, and experience. It's important to find the right coach or consultant who can help you with the right information for your chosen goal. Below is my story about choosing the right coach.

*** Hire the Right Coach—Years ago I needed to renew a license for my career. I knew my weak point and hired someone to coach me to be better. Unfortunately, the person wasn't knowledgeable enough and I failed that part of the exam. Before I would retake the exam I searched for a different teacher. The moment we started talking, I knew this person had the right experience and was the right person to coach me. I passed the exam with flying colors and received my license. It was an important and expensive lesson in choosing a knowledgeable coach who can help you succeed.*

13. Patience, Persistence, and Motivation: Like all things worth pursuing in life, creating a new *self-image or ideal you* takes time and effort. If you take steps every day toward your Spiritually guided goals, you'll be that much farther along than if you hadn't taken any steps. You'd eventually be a year or more older without any progress. Just like a person who wants to reduce their weight or build muscle ... motivate yourself to take daily action, be patient with yourself, and stay persistent in your efforts. You'll soon see progress.

14. Keep a Journal for Various Goals: Journaling can be a powerful tool for self-reflection and personal growth. Write about your journey, your progress, and the positive changes you notice in yourself. Take notes on any ideas that come to you while writing. They may be useful in the future.

15. Journal on any Topic: Write in an "Abundance Journal" because it continues to remind you of how abundant life is for everyone.

"It's easy to take an abundant life for granted and not remember how gratitude and/or appreciation multiplies itself."

At the end of each day I would list all the abundant things that happened for me. That list grew, and over time I recognized that each day became more and more abundant. The people, places, and things I desired and deserved multiplied.

Remember that personal growth, self-improvement, and transformation are ongoing processes. Be kind to yourself and others. Stay committed to your vision of a more successful and empowered self. With dedication, persistence, and a positive mindset, you can make significant shifts in your thought patterns and create your ideal self-image.

Tools for Your Personal Growth

Note the words or phrases you say to yourself that are not empowering! Shift your thought patterns by *replacing negative thoughts with positive affirming thoughts*. How can you be more positive, thoughtful, courageous, or helpful?

*** Surrender—A negative ego-dum trait is like a wild stallion that calls to be disciplined by you. Any competitive sport can be a metaphor for courage and discipline, including the All-American Rodeo. If you've ever been to a rodeo you know it's a competition between a trained rider and a wild horse.

The experienced rider carefully settles onto the already saddled horse behind the gate where assistants try to calm the unsuspecting stallion. The fearful horse finds the saddle uncomfortable and the addition of a heavy rider irritates the horse even more. Once they leave the gate, the untrained horse does its best to buck the rider off his back. If the rider proves his skills of strength, agility, and perseverance, the horse surrenders its fear of the unknown and allows the rider to be his master ... controlling every move the horse makes.*

Develop Courage and Discipline

A Course in Miracles, a self-study training for students to become Miracle-Minded, says that your mind is untrained and undisciplined. One of the goals of *The Workbook Lessons* is to change that. You might think of your mind as comparable to a wild stallion ... in fear of the unknown. To achieve the goal of happiness and harmony at work or at home, you'll need to master your thoughts and understand your emotions. Doing so will solve your conflicts and help you determine if you're following your heart and soul or not.

Watch your thoughts like a hawk until you train yourself to stay away from negative habits such as judgments, grievances, and control ... three blocks that keep love and happiness away. All three blocks fall under the umbrella of fear and work against your joy en mass. I'm not saying it's easy. It takes the skills of constant discipline, strength, and perseverance. If you want to be truly happy and peaceful, those are the rules!

"Whatever you dream you can do, begin it. Boldness has genius, power, and magic in it. Begin it now!" – Johann Wolfgang von Goethe

Inspiration: Intuition and Imagination

Intuition and Imagination are your two inner "I's." You have two outer eyes for seeing in the physical world. And now you've got me telling you about your two inner I's, who bring new discoveries from your inner world to your outer world.

Let's remember that your Higher Power is not necessarily experienced through your five senses. In my experience your psychic and creative connections are accessed through your intuition and imagination ... your 6th and 7th senses. According to my research there are theoretically about 20+ senses. That is beyond the scope of this book and pretty much unnecessary to one's Ideal Life Path unless it's your course of study.

Your five human senses: sight, sound, smell, taste, and touch are perfect for navigating this physical world, but are less important in the Spiritual world. Inner sight and/or visions and hearing sounds of music or your Guide's inner Voice mostly enters your inner experiences ... such as your night time dreams or meditations.

To navigate the Spiritual world of your Higher Power you'll need to develop, if you haven't already, your two spiritual senses: intuition/knowing and imagination/images. Note that I called them your two Inner "I's." *Think of your intuition and imagination like eyes looking inward* ... to see within and what has not yet manifested in your outer world. Your astute awareness and development of those two senses will play a big part in learning your Ideal Life Path.

Don't dismiss what you can't see. You can't see radio waves, but you can hear music and conversation the instant you plug in and turn on a radio. Turn on your Spiritual channel and you'll have more profound inner experiences. Many metaphysical and Miracle-Minded students have reported their experiences: hearing music, an inner Voice, seeing inner images, surprising creativity, much sought after inner guidance, and insightful Spiritual experiences. And it's all natural! That's the best part ... no drugs or alcohol!!

The real Ruler is your Higher Power and its Kingdom of love, peace, and understanding. Once you're awakened to who you really are, *a Spiritual being having a human experience,* and live as though you believe it, the real Kingdom takes shape in your mind, heart, and experiences. It takes a certain amount of insight and discipline to stay in this zone and reap the benefits of connecting with your Higher Power. You'll find that it's worth every small effort, especially once you learn your Ideal Life Path.

Let's take a look at how forces came together to slow down humanity and inspire change.

*** 2020 Vision: The Year of Change—An unexpected worldwide pandemic shifted everybody's life for better or for worse! A perfect example played out in the year 2020 with the Covid 19 pandemic lockdowns. It gave locked down Americans the opportunity to take a major pause in their lives. Unable to reach and/or care for the many family and friends who were sick and dying, Americans were required to live in isolation and slow down their lives. The heart-breaking devastation of becoming ill and dying of the deadly Covid 19 was a real threat to everyone and dramatically changed lives.

Those detrimental circumstances allowed working individuals to get off the treadmill and look at their lives more closely. Experiencing the unexpected 20-20 Vision became an ideal opportunity for change or for creating a personal vision. That introspection caused some people to quit their jobs to pursue a line of work that was more in alignment with their Dreams. Others decided not go back to a suffocating workplace, but to work from home or from a distance where freedom was possible.

The American media named it The Great Resignation. It gave many people an opportunity to acknowledge that they didn't like or feel passionate about their work or co-workers. Many discovered the appeal of spending more time with family. And of course there were those who preferred to spend less time with family.

Those who stayed with uninspiring jobs or careers rebelled by keeping their jobs but quietly retreated from performing at a higher level … and we now call that *"quiet quitting. "*

Masses of people making serious life changes may have been a big step in the dawning of The Great Awakening, called for by the Miracle-Minded and the book, *A Course in Miracles.* This is what we call waking up to who we really are … brave spirits who choose to be in alignment with our Ideal Life Path.

In the aftermath of the 2020 lockdowns people came away with new perspectives about the fragility of life as well as what it means to follow your heart. Once vaccines lessened the chances of people dying from Covid 19, Americans suddenly preferred to spend quality time with their families or live life on their own terms.*

Slow Down First to Speed Up

You don't need a worldwide pandemic to show you what's valuable in life. Slow down your activities and give yourself time to experience what's happening in your life ... your discomfort or miserable situation. That brief time of checking in with yourself could give you insight and clarity about whether you're on the right path or not. I've always felt that it's best to get your head on straight before you start the next chapter of your life. Don't let it be a reflection of a miserable past.

A Tool for Your Personal Growth

How did the 2020 lockdown inspire you to slow down and seek a new life path or shift your perspective on the path you currently travelled? Speed up by becoming aware of what's important to you and take daily action toward Spirit-inspired goals. What is important to you? Use this space to write about your experiences and how you handled the situation.

- How did the 2020 lockdown inspire you to shift your perceptions?
- What's important to you?
- What daily actions can you take?
- How did you handle difficulties at that time?
- How do you handle them now?

Search Your Soul for Meaningful Answers

- Mindfulness and honoring yourself are important skills to learn.
- Slow down and learn to be mindful of when it's time for a change or to seek for something more.
- Always honor what you're feeling in the moment, especially emotions of anxiety.
- When uncomfortable moments start piling up, you're no longer honoring who you are and what you want for your life.

- Identify red flags or heart-related signals of frustration in your life or career.
- Be mindful about the onset of physical pain. Shoulder and neck pain are usually signs of stress.

Tools for Your Personal Growth

You think you don't know what you want regarding your life direction? But what if you DID know? What would that be? Close your eyes and ask what calls to you in this moment?

A Heart Centering Visualization

The guided imagery session below is intended to help you discover your Ideal Life Path, although it may or may not be revealed the first time through. You may receive guidance a day or two later. You can always return to this visualization and do it again. Read through this visualization a couple of times before you go on this heart-opening journey:

Explore Your Heart—Your Truth!

Close your eyes. Take a few deep breaths. Breathe in, hold, let go, and take two more deep breaths. (Do a brief body scan.) Relax your muscles from your feet to the top of your head. Name each body part as you ask it to relax. (Example: *"I feel all the muscles in my toes and feet begin to unwind and relax." "I move that relaxed and comfortable feeling up into the calf muscles, knees, and thighs."*) Continue naming muscles all the way to the top of your head. Take your time.

Find your way into your heart muscle. Relax into it for a minute. Continue to breathe and watch it pump your life force, the blood that carries precious oxygen throughout your body. Slow down your pace and watch it flow.

Imagine that you have the power to change that life force into sacred and healing energy. As you breathe into it, it takes on a beautiful soft golden light pulsing through your veins and arteries.

As you enter your heart notice what your heart looks like, not a physical heart, but lovely and vibrant four chambers pulsing with your sacred energy: love, wisdom, and truth sending nurturing light throughout your body. Allow your unique energies to flow and swirl through you and around you. Call the energy by name: "Love, Wisdom, and Truth, Love, Wisdom, and Truth!"

Ask your question several times, *"What does my soul want?"* or *"What can I do (who can I be?) that's in my own best interests?" "What truth does my heart want me to know?"* Allow your heart some time to respond. What is your heart telling you? Wait a few minutes then thank your heart for how it serves you, loves you, and keeps you healthy.

When you're ready, give yourself a few minutes to return back into the room. Stand and stretch your body out. Write down your experience.

Your Next Steps

This chapter invites you to enter a new paradigm, one that establishes your true Identity as a Spirit having a human experience. It offers you a roadmap for becoming the person your Higher Power would have you be. Here is a reminder of how to get there: believe in yourself, create powerful intentions and use the fifteen recommendations (not all at once), to set your intentions. Develop courage and discipline and always use your intuition and imagination (that still small voice) to navigate your way in the world. And finally, use the Heart Centering Visualization to connect with the truth within your heart.

CHAPTER SIX

EMBRACE THE POSSIBILITIES

The last few chapters helped you shift into a new identity. You've worked on your fears, limitations, triggers, and patterns. You cleared away everything but the faith leading to your destiny. The Miracle-Minded understand, "a miracle paves the way for ... love's awakening." (ACIM wkbk.Part II.13)

In this chapter you'll build on your newfound vision of yourself, a Spirit having a human experience. A loving new identity to bring on new and rewarding opportunities, possibilities and responsibilities. Just know that your world is about to change. When you change your mind about who you are, you'll embrace the loving future meant for you.

Dream BIG!

Step 1: It's entire possible that you have a particular Dream due to your Higher Power planting a seed of destiny. If you're still unsure of your guidance yet, set your intentions on your Dreams and what might help them manifest. If doors open, you're on the right path. If not, you may need to keep asking for inner Guidance.

Do you need a positive mindset, a dynamic or humorous personality, additional education, or an awareness of your values, etc? Start now to *call in* something you deeply desire and seek the possibilities. The Universe wants you to dream big Dreams so it may create a more dynamic Earth, bringing in heavenly qualities. (Thy Kingdom come, thy will be done on Earth as it is in Heaven.)

Step 2: Embrace the Possibilities and Freedom. Embracing the possibilities and opportunities for growth are the path forward for your good, your light, and your destiny. Take what goodness and valuable lessons you've learned, but leave the sad stuff behind ... including your mistakes. Taking them will weigh on you and you'll never know what you could have been or done. If you don't have a sense of freedom yet, go back to the past chapters and use the Tools For Personal Growth. As you ready yourself to do your Higher Power's will for you, know that doors will open, opportunities present themselves, and His light will shine on you. What can you leave behind? What can you embrace?

Step 3: Acceptance is a BIG Wow! You're Miracle-Minded! Accepting this new Identity gives you advantages (or superpowers) that are not in another's awareness.

Step 4. Build a foundation: use your strengths, your Higher Power's strength ... and the Success Skills you'll learn in this coaching program. Your foundation is patience, awareness, persistence, faith, or trust for you to see your own light and the light in others.

Set up four structural pillars for more confidence:

1. Spirit support: Look within for support through inner listening.
2. Mindfulness/listening: Make time for reflection and introspection.
3. Perseverance: Stay with your commitment to learn your true path.
4. Courage: Your faith and trust will overcome any fears that arise.

Step 5. Place your Ideal Life Path (once you know it) on top of all you've learned about yourself and your future ... and go for it!

SUCCESS SKILLS

The success skill for this journey is trust. Trust in yourself and in your Higher Power. Trust everyone who's come before you who revealed that their courage came from believing in themselves and trusting the Universe. It takes two and you're not alone.

Embrace a "Possibility" Mindset

When embarking on the journey to discover your Ideal Life Path, the concept of "Embrace the Possibilities" serves as a foundational mindset. It means opening yourself to the many paths and opportunities that life presents, each offering unique lessons and experiences essential for your personal growth. It involves cultivating a sense of curiosity, wonder, and openness to new experiences, ideas, and perspectives.

As you seek to learn your Ideal Life Path, embracing possibilities allows you to step beyond your comfort zone and explore uncharted territories. This exploration is not limited to grand, life-changing events but also includes the small, everyday moments that contribute to your understanding of who you are and what you're here to do. By embracing possibilities, you acknowledge that your purpose may evolve over time and that each experience, whether positive or negative, adds a valuable piece to the beautiful puzzle of your life's journey.

In practical terms, embracing possibilities involves several key actions. First, it means adopting a growth mindset, where challenges are viewed as opportunities for learning rather than obstacles. This perspective encourages you to take risks that might seem daunting at first. Second, it requires a willingness to let go of rigid expectations and be flexible in your approach.

As I previously mentioned, life's path is rarely a straight line, but an interesting maze. Being adaptable allows you to navigate the twists and turns with grace and resilience. It also involves a commitment to continuous self-discovery. Regular reflection, meditation, and self-assessment help you stay attuned to your inner Voice. It ensures that your actions align with your evolving sense of purpose and/or your Higher Power's will for you.

A Tool for Your Personal Growth—The Welcome Mat

Rather than engaging in New Year's resolutions, which you most likely forget about a month later, focus on what you want to welcome into your life in the current year. It's like a welcome mat you set out in front of an open door (For your Dreams). Imagine you are welcoming your Dreams or Ideal Life Path into your life. State three things, situations, or experiences you would welcome into your life this year. Write them here:

1.
2.
3.

Your Next Steps

"Embrace the Possibilities," highlights the importance of maintaining an open and curious mindset as you seek to discover your true purpose. You're encouraged to view life as a dynamic journey filled with potential pathways and opportunities for growth. By adopting a miracle mindset and staying flexible, you can navigate life's challenges and uncertainties. Embracing possibilities empowers you to see each experience as a valuable lesson, helping you piece together the unique puzzle of your life's purpose and ultimately lead you to a more fulfilling and meaningful life.

CHAPTER SEVEN

THE AMAZING POWERS OF YOUR MIND

Let's explore the amazing powers of your mind, because your mind is the breeding ground where your thoughts and perceptions come together for you. They lead you to take action toward learning your purpose or not. I think of the mind and its thoughts as middle ground ... a neutral area where ideas can be pushed or pulled in one direction or another. Thoughts or ideas pop into your head from seemingly nowhere. No one really knows how that works and it's complicated. Thoughts come from somewhere, possibly the subconscious or super-conscious mind. Some scientists think your thoughts and actions originate from your past experiences.

Metaphysicians believe they originate through your Higher Power or perhaps from the ethers. Or your ego might jump in and hijack original thoughts for its own selfish purposes. All of these ideas could be right or I could be missing the mark. It actually doesn't matter as long as your thoughts awaken you to the situations or circumstances you need to address. Your mind and its creative powers are truly a unique and interesting laboratory ... right behind your eyes.

Your one decision in this matter is what to do with your creative thoughts as they float around in this neutral middle ground. If you think of your mind as a laboratory, then it becomes an experimental place for mixing and measuring thoughts and ideas. You have two choices ... you can ignore them or follow and act on them. It's an important decision and you must either use trial and error, and/or trust them. For my part, I often relied on a combination of intuition, common sense, and discernment to make those decisions, depending on the goal at hand.

Your Higher Power Versus Your Mind Power

I'd like to share two concepts, both of which are totally natural. The first concept is the domain of your Higher Power. It's about following intuition, your still small inner Voice, or the Divine Guidance of your higher Self or Higher Power. I don't claim to know the perfect answer or an always-correct way to do it. I only know what works for me, and the many people I've interviewed over the years—many of which were Miracle-Minded. I believe you'll find it both valuable and interesting.

For me, the Voice is unmistakable. That's why I place my focus and importance on the Divine inner Voice. I'll go further into that idea in this chapter and in upcoming chapters.

You can also read my other book, *"The Art of Listening to Your Heart and Soul: Awaken to Your Intuition and Inner Guidance."*

It's easy to misinterpret your intuition, hunches, or assumptions. That doesn't mean intuitions etc. are meaningless. No, there's a place for them in all circumstances, so go with your gut or heart or common sense by thinking through your intuitions, actions, and their repercussions. Learn to trust in your own inner wisdom. I learned quickly through trial and error ... especially the error part.

I've heard it said that *'the mind is a better servant than it is a master.'* So the goal is to *master your mind* so it becomes a servant to you and your Higher Power. Affirmations, visualizations, mindset tools for personal growth, and positive thinking are effective ways to make the mind your servant.

What about your human powers? The Miracle-Minded know that their most important superpower is that of *decision*. Another superpower is your *willingness* and ability to use your decisions for your Higher Power's will when it's revealed to you.

The second concept is about using the three parts of your mind: conscious, subconscious, and super-conscious, to create experiences and to solve problems. (Some chapters are about solving or healing personal problems and others are about the creative experience.) The big mystery is that there appears to be an overlap between the two domains.

Learning to access all three parts of your mind: conscious, subconscious, and super-conscious, is to mine valuable information that can give you insight into the Divine plan for your life! You'll get more specific Spiritual Guidance to speed up the process, depending on how close you are in time to learning your destiny.

1. Your Conscious Mind is what you're using right now and you use it daily to navigate your way in the world. To the Miracle-Minded your conscious mind is always in touch with and listening to your Higher Power ... except when your ego speaks louder. *A Course in Miracles* says we are to hear the inner Voice all throughout the day. Complete mindfulness is the best way to accomplish that.

You commonly refer to the conscious mind as your daytime 'awake' mind. You'll use it to navigate your worldly experience and it helps you to be conscious of everything happening to and around you on a daily basis. You may believe what your conscious mind and your five senses tell you is your reality. Metaphysically speaking, that's not true. The conscious mind is really *the sleeping mind.* You're asleep to who you really are ... a Spiritual being having a human experience.

The Sleeping Mind

The Miracle-Minded believe that the mind is spiritually asleep to the internal power it possesses and its sacred connection to its Divine Source. You must be awakened to this fact. And oddly enough, your ego is actually opposed to and threatened by the idea of being awakened to its Divinity. Why? Because of its misunderstanding and misperceptions: fear of the unknown and a loss of personal power. In a nutshell, that fear and loss causes a belief in separation from your Higher Power and feelings of guilt for trying to usurp It's Divine Power. A Spiritual Awakening shifts both of these misperceptions and you return to your Divine nature ... Love.

The conscious/perceptual and sleeping mind may not perceive your Higher Power to be the loving, benevolent Being it is. You can diminish that fear by embracing and trusting your Higher Power, i.e. the God of your heart. You've been told throughout time to fear a wrathful, vengeful God. That absurd idea is totally unwarranted!

You are chosen as a co-creator on this Earth and your Higher Power depends on you to activate His will. It's my purpose to share this message with you. By not activating His will you are actually mis-creating through your faulty beliefs. This basically means you're fighting it!

*"No problem can be solved from the same level of consciousness that created it. "*Albert Einstein, Scientist and Philosopher

The solution to mis-creating (separation from your Source) is by connecting with your Higher Power on the mental and spiritual level to discover your Higher Power's solution ... the only solution that matters. The next chapter can help you shift into your listening mode.

2. Your Subconscious Mind is where all learning takes place and memories are stored. It's like a basement or storage area. This part of your mind is what you'll access when you want to learn something new and remember it later or retrieve something you learned long ago. You may be able to retrieve words and ideas you learned in your youth.

3. Your Super-Conscious Mind, which is also called the Universal Mind, is the most powerful part of your mind. It's an area that knows your past, present, and future and is your most powerful resource and ally.

If you have an innate need to learn and attain your destiny, this is the area of mind where you'll receive your guidance, as best you can. You can reach this state during sleep, deep meditation, or possibly slip into it during quiet times throughout your day. Your inner direction comes from your super-conscious mind/your Higher Power, not your ego or someone else's direction. You can choose to ignore it or follow through on what you hear or feel.

4. Your Imagination: All three parts of your mind are the imagining factor. You're able to internally create or receive images and project them onto the screen of your world. In other words, you have a powerful imagination.

The Law of Attraction is a basic Universal law of cause and effect and uses your imagination as a tool for manifestation. You get back what you put out ... if it's meant for you. In my experience, my requests are often satisfied when I focus within first, then ask with sincerity and feeling/emotion. I often use affirmations, visualizations, and mental rehearsal.

Reflections and Mirrors

Metaphysically speaking, the world is an out picturing of what's in your mind. It can be a reflection of your thoughts and perceptions or your Dreams and fantasies ... if you acted on them. You'll see what you want to see.

Be mindful of "projection." It's a psychological term that states, 'what's true about you is projected onto someone else,' positive or negative. Because you are seeing it, that person or entity is showing you (mirroring you) where *you* are the cause of the judgment or association. It's as true in the political realm as it is in your workplace or home life.

In order to get the support of your subconscious and super-conscious mind, you'll *find your power in asking with an open heart and mind.* Be ready to listen and receive.

According to ACIM the Miracle-Minded are to pray for *some kind of experience* rather than make a laundry list of demands. You may request *"the experience of romantic love"* or *"the experience of abundance"* or "the experience of right livelihood," while leaving the details (the how?) up to your Higher Power. Read my story below, *"Get Yourself a Social Life."* It's an example of how that played out in my life.

*** Get Yourself A Social Life—I was lonely, so I once prayed for the experience of a more vibrant social life. I quickly went from a long period of quiet times to a dramatically busy social life. It changed so rapidly and radically that I exclaimed to my ACIM friends with an exhausted voice, *"be careful what you ask for!"* We all chuckled about my new dilemma.*

Own Your Superpowers:
Awaken to Your Intuition and Imagination

The main reason to awaken to your creative intuition (sixth sense) and imagination (seventh sense) is to be able to align and co-create with your Higher Power in a way that's productive to Its plan and yours. Intuition means inner learning and/or knowing. Most anyone can learn from books. It takes a different skill set to learn Spiritual processes and development. This coaching program is meant to help you learn and receive knowledge from a higher form of intelligence. ... your Higher Power. It's not artificial—It's the real deal.

Imagination is accessing your imagining capabilities. Developing this skill or superpower has immense value in this world and to society: inventions, innovations, science-based, and creativity in the arts. Your paintings, writings, poetry, songs, speeches come through you and may achieve a genius level. No one knows how that works and why some people attain genius status and others do not. I do know that intuition and imagination are true superpowers that all can access.

You awaken to your creative talents by understanding that you have a Spiritual knowing and power, but it may be sleeping within you. Awakening your intuition is a process of learning that your Higher Power is real, even though your five senses don't reveal this truth. It's through your faith in the sixth and seventh senses that it becomes most useful for you. You'll connect with these two senses through the tools in each chapter asking you to become more focused.

Your intuitive sixth sense allows you to know information that you may not have been taught. You'll have automatic insights into people, situations, and circumstances that other people are not aware of.

Imagination is another profound mental and Spiritual ability. Someone in touch with their imaginary senses have access to ideas, images, and creations from beyond the physical world. Imagination doesn't always develop on it's own. I discovered that you may have to encourage it by focusing/thinking about what is possible, read books or take classes on creativity. Take part in practice exercises, games, or brainstorm with people who appear to have a creative connection on your topics of interest.

Beyond listening for inner intuitive guidance, you might be inspired to add to your skills like I did in my first story of allowing my guidance to direct me. My Higher Power didn't teach me graphic design, but those He inspired to teach were my mentors. They activated their Higher Powers' will for them. I learned the basics through books and classes. I did not automatically know the computer or graphic design when I went to college. I was guided, like my classmates.

Get into alignment with what you want to accomplish: painting, business, marketing, creative writing, or holistic health etc., by learning the steps, processes, and systems from those who've already done it. Just like this Learn Your Life Purpose course, you're learning the steps, processes, and systems from my lifelong experiences as a clairaudient person.

My Higher Power led me to this path so I could teach it to you. I planned to write a meditation book but my Higher Power sent me in this direction. So here I am. Your Higher Power leads you to creative endeavors to be used within His plan.

By studying the systems and processes you become a magnet and attract to you the ideas and wisdom for whatever you're guided to accomplish. Once you are immersed, focused, and in alignment, the ideas and images come to you normally with very little difficulty, yet it's the execution that may take a while. Like Albert Einstein said, *"Creativity is 1% inspiration and 99% perspiration."* I can attest to that fact.

The important thing to remember is to not be afraid. Trust that in the right and perfect time and circumstances, your art form will successfully manifest for you. You'll be ready for your Dreams or Ideal Life Path.

Obviously there are geniuses, such as Mozart, Leonardo de Vinci, Albert Einstein, Nikola Tesla, Marie Curie, Thomas Edison, and others who naturally attract the right and perfect art form.

Use the amazing powers of your mind: conscious, subconscious, and super-conscious, to focus on Guidance leading to clues about your Ideal Life Path. At the same time use your meditation practice to get into alignment with your Higher Power. There's a lesson in ACIM that says, *"I will step back and let Him lead the way."* Simply trust that He will lead you correctly because your Higher Power's plan needs your willingness, wisdom, values, personality, character, and intelligence. Don't hold back what you're asked to give! You have an important part in your Higher Power's plan.

Your Mental-Spiritual Antenna and Funnel
The three parts of your mind, your conscious, subconscious and your superconscious mind, act like an antenna to your Higher Power. Each one is important in attracting information and keeping your daily life in alignment with the Divine Plan for your life.

You may or may not be aware of it, but you are always being groomed for the part you'll play in the Divine Plan. Here is a story of how I accessed my invisible antenna to co-create a fiction novel, something I never thought I could do. To me, this was a miracle.

*** **Download A Fiction Novel**—I had a creative idea for a fantasy novel. It was my first experience with writing full-length fiction. I took a short story I wrote in a college class and tried to make it a fantasy fiction novel. The goal was to write 50,000 words over a 30 day period of time. I wrote it for National Novel Writing Month (better known as NANOWRIMO). It's a competition each November 1st. I finally gave up at 35,000 words due to structural issues. I was determined to try again the following year and write another romantic fantasy novel. This time I prepared myself.

I studied a book on structure and on my second try I surprisingly seemed to connect with something beyond myself. From the beginning to the end, I felt totally aligned with my Higher Power. My brain or intuition became a funnel, downloading the various parts of the story from the ethers through my mind and fingers onto my computer screen. As I became focused on different aspects of the novel, my subconscious mind would supply me with ideas, images, and insight to continue the novel through to completion. It proved to me how the powers of my mind and a supernatural flow supported me every step of the way!*

I've known authors who share that sometimes the story writes itself or characters interact with them to tell their own story. I'm reminded of the interview with Lin Manual Miranda who wrote the blockbuster rap musical, "Hamilton." He reported that, *"The spirit of Alexander Hamilton grabbed me and wouldn't let me go until I told his story."* Alexander Hamilton's musical life story was a huge success on Broadway, in books, and beyond. Lin Manual Miranda made a powerful connection with his imagination.

* It's important to verbally ask to be led and supported by that wise part of yourself. It's the super-conscious mind/Spirit who knows the Plan of Awakening and where your strengths would be most helpful. Take time to listen for answers.

SUCCESS SKILLS

The necessary skill here is keeping an open mind about having an open mind. There are three aspects of your mind operating at the same time and they're all helping you to be awake to who you really are. You are always acting out your Soul's Purpose through your awareness of: your Divinity, how you're showing up in the world, your alertness to outside influences, and being functional. It's a lot to juggle, but don't get bogged down by this. It should come natural.

Tools for Your Personal Growth

Tool #1: Create an "asking statement." Make up your own request statement or use the one provided:

"Wise part of myself, I sincerely ask for your wisdom and guidance to lead me to what is mine in truth. Please lead me along the path where I may be of service to the world, and in return provide to me a life of prosperity, abundance, peace, perfect happiness, love, and creative self-expression."

Tool #2: Ask your inner Guide or Super-Conscious Mind—this is a shorter version during a Body Scan: *"How would you have me serve?"* What would you have me do?" *"I want to do something meaningful!" "Show me where I can be most helpful!"*

Tool #3: Important: Be patient if you don't receive the answer you're looking for right now. Remember that you've done the asking, so the answer can come at anytime.

Tool #4: Meet Your higher Self

Find some quiet time when it's easy for you to allow your mind and body to slowly relax. Name your body parts: eyes, mouth, jaw, shoulders, etc., from your head to your toes, inviting them to relax. Go within and sink down into a peaceful place, and meet that wise part of yourself. Imagine a wiser YOU appearing before you. You may call that part of you your Higher Self. Once the meeting is established, personally ask that wise part of yourself to guide you on your life journey/path with your Asking Statement.

Then ask if that wise part of yourself has a message or a gift for you? Be patient and wait until you receive it. Thank your wise Self for participating. End your session by counting up from one to five, feeling more energy in your body as you count up. At number five, open your eyes and stretch your arms and body. Take a few minutes to reflect on your experience. You may not have an image right away, but whatever you're feeling or sensing is valid.

Your Next Steps

You've read about the three parts of your mind, how they work, and how to go to a deeper state of mind. These are the states that bring about a more clear connection with your Higher Power. Use the tools to establish your next breakthrough. Next you are going to learn about Inner Listening. You'll take your knowledge of your mind and put it to use by actively listening to your Higher Power.

"Trust that your soul has a plan and even if you can't see it all, know that everything will unfold as it is meant to." Deepak Chopra, M.D. and bestselling author

CHAPTER EIGHT

THE A.R.T. OF INNER LISTENING

The Art of Listening is the cornerstone of this program. In the following chapters we'll talk about meditation, connecting, aligning, and co-creating with your Higher Power. This is where the rubber meets the road. Through inner listening your total mind; conscious, subconscious, and super-conscious mind connect and receive guidance from your Higher Power on how to learn your Ideal Life Path and solve other issues.

The Miracle-Minded believe that you should be able to hear the Voice of your Higher Power all throughout your day. It's possible and I've done it with some success. It requires two things from you: practicing mindfulness by slowing down enough to be able to hear to your Higher Power or inner Teacher and secondly, carry out your daily activities at the same time. After all, one must care for children, drive safely, prepare meals, and more!

WHY IS THIS IMPORTANT?

Inner listening is also outer listening. Once you've mastered the skill of shutting out your ego thoughts and your struggles with the world and have achieved a level of "mindfulness," you'll apply that skill to listening to what you're hearing in the outer world. This might mean interactions, conversations, and energies from the people you interact with. Listening and responding mindfully will allow you to hear what is spoken and unspoken. This leaves you with the important option to ask deeper questions as you gain more clarity.

"In quietness are all things answered, and is every problem quietly resolved." ACIM T.27.IV

Set Your Cornerstone

There are two aspects to going inward to listen and receive Spiritual guidance. One aspect is an A.R.T. and the other a science. We'll be using the artful aspect of Inner Listening because A.R.T. is not only creative but is the most proactive and useful for what we need ... to learn of your Ideal Life Path! I think of quiet listening and mindfulness meditation as cornerstones of the healing arts. It's due to their important potential to heal your body and your mind. It works whether you sit quietly or you move mindfully. It's a powerful process for a connection with your next steps.

In the A.R.T. of Inner Listening, I use the A for Activate, R for Receptivity, and T for Trust. *The "A" stands for Activate.* Your quiet, undistracted subconscious mind is the sacred place where you meet your inner Guide and do some serious listening, leading to activating and co-creating your Ideal Life Path. A large part of the activation process is to avoid distractions. You would turn down the volume on your cell phone, TV, or computer to have a conversation with a friend. In the same vein you would shut off your inner chatter (monkey mind) so you could hear or turn UP the volume of your sacred inner Voice, intuition, and imagination.

The "R" in A.R.T. stands for Receive or Receptivity. When you put yourself in a place of receptivity you'll more easily open your heart and mind to receive everything that is meant for you. It's a real value. You'll connect with your Higher Power or Inner Teacher to hear the sacred guidance and direction that is your true pathway. Without that connection you'll likely struggle to find your way. Realign your focus to put your Higher Power first, not last or as a last resort when all else has failed! Living your Dreams or Ideal Life Path depends on you to relax your body and mind in order to release your fears and judgments. Release your past and current frustrations to discover Divinely inspired direction from a higher level of consciousness.

The "T" in A.R.T. stands for Trust. Your responsibility is to trust in your Higher Power. There is no other authority that can guide you to your ultimate Ideal Life Path than your higher Self, i.e. connection with your Higher Power. You may not be comfortable or confident enough to blindly follow an inner Voice. That is understandable and why I suggest reprogramming your mind to follow a path you can trust, which for me is *A Course in Miracles.*

I encourage you to train your mind to let go of what doesn't serve you, ego-dum misperceptions, and trust in what does ... your Higher Power's plan for you. I personally trained in the teachings of ACIM and learned to surrender my will for my Higher Power's will. You may find another Spiritual path of your choosing that resonates with your belief system.

Your commitment is not just to listen inwardly but to use it as a bridge to discover 'what it takes' to live your Dreams. Your inner Guide knows that information.

Trust your Higher Power to lead you to what does serve you, which is a future you want and is meant to be! That is accomplished through active listening and taking action when requested.

Transcend or rise up over any fears that your Higher Power may lead you astray. Since you don't know what the future holds, a certain amount of trust and courage are needed. Use The A.R.T. of Listening to co-create the life of your Dreams.

"Activate, Receive, and Trust that you can uphold your part of the plan."

Maybe you'll receive guidance that seems out of sorts to you! Instead of following it you can say, *"no!"* and let it go that. I've done that … I said, *"sorry, but no"* to Spirit when it was suggested I move so soon after an expensive move. You may not feel comfortable with jumping in on something … and you'll never know what could have been. Fear and its partner, the unknown, are huge roadblocks to Spiritual achievement. I'm sharing this to say that the same guidance may come around at another time and instead of saying *"no"* you'll be ready to say *"yes!"* as circumstances change.

On the other hand, I've learned that when Guidance wants you to do something necessary it will present its request in various ways and whatever is needed to get you to do it. It's non-negotiable!!

*** **Expansion**—After I completed this book, *Learn Your Life Purpose,* I wrote another book to expand upon this chapter: *"The ART of Listening to Your Heart and Soul; Awaken to Your Intuition and Divine Inner Guidance."**

Prepare a Strong Personal Foundation

I've talked about preparing a strong personal foundation for your journey to self-awareness, the knowledge of your Ideal Life Path, and perhaps even your Spiritual Awakening. Inner listening is about building that strong foundation for a more deeply personal relationship with your Higher Power

Inner listening is designed to give you six solid instructions on how to empty your mind of useless thoughts from your past in order to create an empty container for new, wiser thoughts to enter. I call this your wise inner Voice. You'll follow your trusted Spiritual Guide to a better life and future.

Active Listening can become a balancing act for prayer and meditation. Metaphysically speaking, prayer is for speaking to your Higher Power and meditation is for listening to Guidance and directions. When you aren't able or willing to listen or hear your inner Teacher/Guide, guidance subtly comes to you by other forms of communication: dreams, conversations, intuition, books etc. Tap into any of these ways to evolve your Spiritual awareness.

*** Your First Inner Voice Experience—Like myself, you'll always remember your first experience of hearing your wise inner Resource. This very personal and life changing story impacted my young and future life in unexpected ways. When I was around 4 or 5 years old, I was lured into a situation that had the potential to be traumatizing. In the middle of it all, I heard a male inner Voice inside my head that instructed me how to protect myself from an adult who, unbeknownst to me, intended to sexually molest me. I did as the Voice instructed and was able to stop the perpetrator.*

In that very moment I learned about a wise inner Resource and by listening to that guidance, how it could help me in times of need, and during turning points in my adult life. Instead of becoming a victim, I could choose to be the victor and my Higher Power would always be my support system!

Later in life I worked on myself through personal growth classes, trainings, books, and recordings to further develop my listening skills. I understood that it was first, a gift and secondly, a skill that would serve me the rest of my life. I would slow down and be mindful so I could access that wise inner guidance, allowing it to guide and direct my decisions and actions. I trust that you'll gain inspiration from my unexpected first personal experience.

Six Takeaways from The A.R.T. of LISTENING!

1. A personal connection with your own Inner Wisdom or what the Miracle-Minded call the higher Self: that childlike part of yourself who is open to learning, who is innocent, and courageous enough to take those first steps toward a new life path.

2. A strong willingness to listen within and act on your guidance or intuition from what metaphysically minded people call the Spirit or Universal Mind (God of your heart, Your Higher Power, the Divine), which we are all part of. Sometimes you may not be aware of an Inner Voice or receive inner images. That's okay! Let your intuition decide if what you are sensing is valid. It knows which direction to go that's in your own best interests. You'll soon learn that if a door doesn't open, it's not the right door for you.

3. Be mindful of the thoughts and perceptions that come to you. They will most likely feel or sound different than your own voice and offer wise or friendly advice. Remember that your Higher Power's messages can be subtly repetitive, non-intrusive, sometimes surprising, and will guide you wisely.

4. Slow down, take your time, and be more mindful of everything you do. Much of the world wants to do everything faster, but faster is not always the best solution when it comes to living your precious life. Slowing down gives the very subtle intuition an opportunity to lead the way, rather than you rushing around with your own chaotic plans.

Slowing down can help you to be in the right place at the right time. You would meet someone you need to meet or learn a bit of knowledge that couldn't have gotten to you in any other way.

You may experience many happy surprises by living mindfully and tuning in to your awareness before you speak. Miraculous situations or synchronicities easily occur when you shift your mindset from hurried to relaxed! I challenge you to try it out for two weeks or so to experience how your life can change from mindless to magical.

5. Pay attention to Turning Points. You may discover, as I have, that the strongest guidance often comes at the turning points in your life. You may find yourself at an important crossroads. A life changing decision must be made and it's an important moment for you. At these intersections a strong intuition tends to take the lead.

Those turning points and your Higher Power's guidance might happen when you're making critical decisions: about a new job, a health-related surgery, buying or selling a business, a move to a different location, the desire for a child, or a decision regarding a trip or vacation. I've been guided in these areas over the years.

There were also times when I wasn't aware of any Guidance, yet I did the right thing at the right time anyway. It's comforting to know when you're in alignment with the Universe and your destiny. I'll say this over and over ... if your desires don't work out, don't fret, as something else is on its way to you ... and it might be better for you.

6. When you aren't hearing Guidance. There may be long periods of time when you're not aware of any Guidance coming to you and other times when it arrives almost daily. As your situations change, you may or may not need any additional Guidance. Coasting is not a bad thing.

If I don't receive Guidance on a decision, I have to trust that my own wisdom will suffice. I've occasionally been corrected by my inner Guide and needed to reverse a decision. I trusted that it was in my own best interests and it proved to be correct.

There are some situations where you may not get an immediate response from your inner Guide. If not, trust that your intuition and common sense will take over and you'll make the best decision possible. If doors open for you, then trust you've made the right decision. You can apply this system to most any question, even to your Ideal Life Path.

Resolve Your Focus

When I was five years old I heard an inner voice through my innocence and non-judgment childlike presence. As you age and life requires more of you, you sometimes lose that attention to your inner wisdom. A Spiritual practice becomes important to reconnecting with that innocent inner child, inner Voice, and sacred wisdom. "The A.R.T. of LISTENING" is designed to prepare you for the innocence and openness you once enjoyed. Continue to trust again.

*** **Excuses**—For many years I looked out the window, distracted from my work, wishing I were somewhere else. I eventually received Guidance to move to a part of the country that fascinated me. Instead of jumping at the chance, I made other plans and excuses not to go right away. I used what I thought of as 'my common sense' to hold back that experience. Thankfully, Spirit corrected that error a short time later.*

Do you ever make decisions that take you away from your goals? I have and I shared that story in the previous paragraph! Throughout the years I've tried to understand that motivation. It's an odd idea to not choose what would ultimately bring you closer to a Dream or possible happiness.

You can blame it on fear and you can't always know in advance what is good for you, but you can listen and trust your Higher Power to know.

As mentioned in my **Excuses** story, how I ignored the Guidance and later I was strongly encouraged to move across the country. I soon realized to not make that move was not an option. I shifted my thinking and it changed my life by giving me substantial opportunities for a better, more remarkable life.

You can rise above any resistance or negative perceptions by opening your heart and reprogramming your mind to focus on a future you and/or your family deserve. Listen and wait for the emotional joy! Make a mental shift toward the positive aspect of your guidance. Those thoughts and perceptions bear the gifts of a happier future.

It's possible to talk yourself into or out of your transcendent experience, depending on what you think you want. You actually don't know what will help you reach your goals. That's why inner listening is so important.

A Daily Inner Listening Session

Read this simple meditation a couple times before you start: Gently close your eyes and take a few deep breaths. Sink deeply into your breath and a deeper place inside yourself where you feel safe and secure.

Breath in fresh air to expand your lungs ... your inner wings (which are upside down in humans). Three or four breaths turn your wings around so you are ready to soar!

Chant – Chanting or deep breathing helps to strengthen your focus to avoid distraction. You may also chant the word "One" or "OM" which means One. Oneness with your Higher Power is a worthy goal.

Focus on your (invisible) third eye, located on the inside of the bridge of your nose. It faces inward, and allows you (once open) to see what you can't see with your two physical eyes.

Continue to relax and breathe. Allow yourself to let go of trying to accomplish anything. Be aware of a subtle shift in consciousness that happens for you to receive either oral guidance or imagery. It's difficult to explain but you'll recognize the shift when it happens. Over time you may notice a deeper level of awareness. When you're ready, bring your attention back into the room, stretch your body and possibly take notes of your experience.

* Once you have some experience with meditation you can direct your session to accomplish some of your goals. Focus inward to build strength and pursue only goals that are in your own best interests.

Create a Daily Listening Habit

Don't make important decisions for your precious life by the seat of your pants. Create a daily habit of listening to your inner Guidance through your Spiritual practice. If getting insight into your destiny is important to you, there are some important points to remember:

Point #1: If an inner Voice tells you to do something violent or hurtful to yourself or someone else, it is NOT the Voice of your Higher Power. It's your own misguided ego and is sabotaging your life. Do NOT listen to any inner Voice that is negative, critical, judgmental, or destructive in any way. Your Higher Power's guidance has only your own best interests in mind. Always remember that!

Point #2: You don't have to suffer through your brief life on Earth from bad life decisions. You'll make mistakes like everyone else. If you can forgive others for their mistakes, you can surely forgive yourself for yours. You'll look back at some point and think it was not a big deal or you may not even remember what you were upset about. Forgiveness and moving on is the most loving way to heal any discomfort you feel. I'll go more into forgiveness in the Chapter – Adjust Your Halo!

Point #3: Utilize your inner Resources to take despair and suffering to a minimal level. Offer your concerns to your Higher Power and ask for guidance on your next steps. You're human, change is a given, and you'll always be challenged with something unforeseen. A large part of life is *on the job training*. You'll learn, grow, and evolve.

Point #4: Any action you perceive as a mistake may not be a mistake at all. It might even be part of the Divine plan and you'll learn that only in hindsight. Mistakes might be lessons you need to learn … until you get it right or choose correctly. There's a workbook lesson in ACIM that says, *"All things are lessons God would have me learn."* I repeat it to myself when it's appropriate!

Point #5: Unfortunately, some Spiritual Guidance can be cryptic and unclear. I've experienced a bit of frustration, especially with Guidance that comes to me when I'm still half asleep. It's sometimes so quick or illusive that I have no other choice than to dismiss it. Remember to write as much as you can remember in your Sleep Journal.

Point #6: Let's also understand that everyone has different ideas of what would make them happy. No two happy Dreams are alike. Some of you think its money by any means or an addictive lifestyle. Maybe you put your faith in a career to bring you fulfillment? Perhaps you are happy to have a loving, joyful relationship and family life? The great joy of life is that you get to choose … every day … and the results show up for you!

SUCCESS SKILLS

Develop your awareness and Spiritual practice to activate your Creative Intuition or Active Listening skills. It's a quiet opportunity for an inner Voice to guide you on your life journey. You'll build the awareness of a valuable Resource to help you navigate any confusing terrain.

This is your own personal Guidance system to lead you TO your life path and HOW to navigate it once you're aware of it. Remember, the sacred seed is already planted. Your part is to birth it and I'm guiding you toward that experience!

Listening Equals Inner Strength

A promising career and Ideal Life Path can be sidetracked by outside influences. I call this, *"Going From an Outer Vice to an Inner Voice."* The Vice includes any thoughts or activities that take you away from your highest potential. Instead of turning inward to connect with your Higher Power and hear a wise inner Voice, individuals sometimes turn outward to engage in harmful habits, better known as vices. Education is key for correcting poor life decisions.

You are out of balance by over consuming anything that is toxic like a drug; alcohol, tobacco, overeating/obesity, illicit habits – stealing, emotional abuse, sexual abuse, trafficking, or engaging in any dark and negative habits that hurt you or another person. You may think of this as an addiction.

The word "D.R.U.G.S." has a larger meaning: Destructive Relationship Undermining God's Sons. (ACIM uses the term Sons to describe all children of God. It does so to simplify the terms he and she and also as a symbolic term that we are all brothers to Jesus as a Son of God.) Beware of anything that undermines your health, your good, or your Soul's purpose.

If detaching from your inner Spirit got you into trouble in the past or present, then the awareness of that Spirit and/or the awakening of the relationship will correct the problem of separation from it.

The following two stories demonstrate how looking within and letting one's Spiritual practice cause a shift in inner strength.

*** **D.R.U.G.S.**—It was in the early 1970's when the stresses of life had gotten to me: dating and relationships, an overbearing father, and the stresses of a new job. Recreational drugs were popular with so many young people of my generation. Drugs, sex, and rock and roll ... right? I used certain drugs frequently, along with alcohol. I didn't use them any more or less than my circle of friends, but what was initially enjoyable and engaging shifted for me. After some time, it became a nightmare of paranoia and the loss of my will to live. I stopped myself from jumping off the balcony at a rock concert. That's when I knew enough was enough—time to grow up!

For many years I wanted to quit using drugs, but didn't have the inner strength to say, *"NO!"* I wanted to be part of the whole "Summer of Love" vibration going on at the time, even though the paranoia became a soul crushing experience.

The 1970's were also a time of liberation and mind expansion. I was eager to explore those options too. I included an avid daily meditation practice into my life. I was around 26 when I woke up one morning and realized that something shifted inside of me and I was completely sure that I was finished with using drugs.

I hadn't received counseling and I wasn't aware of receiving guidance. At the time my strong commitment seemed to have come out of the blue. Meditation was my daily practice and I credit that practice and my connection with my Higher Power for the inner strength to finally say *"NO!"* I walked around my home and tossed all my smoking supplies and pills, etc. into a bag and gave it away. I never looked back. *

*** Tina Turner—You may remember the movie about the popular singer, Tina Turner, *"What's Love Got to do with it?"* She told a story of her stormy marriage to Ike Turner and how her shift to Buddhist meditation and chanting gave her the inner strength to finally end her unhappy marriage of abuse. She went on to have a triumphant career and happier life.*

Your Next Steps

The A.R.T. of Inner Listening ... activating, receiving, and trusting are prerequisites for success in your relationship with your Higher Power. In this chapter you learned about the A.R.T. of Listening and how it's the cornerstone of your Spiritual practice. It's a step forward in the realization of your Ideal Life Path. Create a daily habit of listening to your inner Voice. In the next chapter you'll lead into another powerful gateway ... mindfulness and Goal-directed Meditation.

CHAPTER NINE

GOAL-DIRECTED MEDITATION

"An open mind is an unobstructed path to freedom!" Linda L. Chappo

To be still and silent at regular intervals is the single most life changing action you can take to open your mental, emotional, and Spiritual gateway. It's been done for thousands of years and that in itself, proves it's holistic value to a mind, body, and Spirit connection. Many call this practice Mindfulness Meditation or simply ... meditation.

Meditation is one of the important gateways to receiving higher guidance, along with your sleep time dreams. Because you live in a very busy environment, the quiet time of meditation and sleep are the most effective way for Spirit to connect with you. You may also receive Guidance during your day while conscious.

Because you're in a relaxed state in meditation or asleep, your inner Voice/Higher Power doesn't meet with mental resistance. Your Higher Power rejuvenates, reprograms, and heals your body and mind according to its plan. At the same time it imparts its messages and wisdom to your mind so you may act accordingly. You can depend on personal experience and the experience of metaphysically minded people for the validity of this information.

As a side note, to address physical healing is beyond the scope of this book. You may address the topic in your meditations and prayers and ask for Guidance.

When you meditate on a daily basis, you subtly enter into a powerfully holy space and a mental agreement that connects you to the Spiritual dimension. In a previous chapter I called it your super-conscious mind. You can reach this amazing dimension over time by being consistent and quieting your distracting thoughts. Hush them away, not giving those distractions any power over you.

There are two main goals for meditation as it applies to learning your Ideal Life Path. The first goal is to pay steady attention to your thoughts and what they are saying to you or about you. Are they positive, negative, neutral? The second goal is to let those thoughts go, be neutral, and stay open to Higher Power's Guidance to fill that space.

Know that anytime you enter into a meditation or silent session, you can enter with or without a personal goal. Goals for meditation can be health benefits, to deepen your Spiritual awareness, and to learn how to keep negative thoughts at bay and/or achieve inner peace. In this case, your goal is to reach your Higher Power and to learn of your Ideal Life Path and/or the steps that will get you there.

WHY IS THIS IMPORTANT?

It's important to take your power back from your ego thoughts that may have a strong hold on you. The purpose of going inward in a goal-directed way is to leave the physical dimension, your despair, and negative thoughts behind. You don't need those distractions. You'll make space for you to enter the dynamic Spiritual dimension where you'll discover in due time: the possibilities, potential, and purpose for which you seek. That's the importance of building a personal foundation through inner listening via mindful meditation as opposed to absent-mindedness.

It's also important to know that through meditation or quiet resonance you are meeting the Spiritual realm on Its turf, not yours! Your Higher Power's turf is not the physical world, but it's the silence, the deep, quiet part of your mind. It's the part that listens and makes space for the awareness of your inner wisdom. Your focused silence, deep and steady breathing, and open mind is the gateway to a connection with Your Higher Power. Over time, that process allows you to co-create a more mindful you and a meaningful life.

Lighten Your Emotional & Mental Burdens

There are mental and emotional benefits of Goal-Directed Meditation You'll find those benefits sprinkled throughout this program. That clearing out of old recycled chatter, known to metaphysical students as *monkey mind,* can unburden your mental and emotional state … allowing you the freedom to choose purposeful thoughts.

Choose the thoughts that take you in the direction you want to go. Don't just spin the old negative thoughts that keep you stuck: how much you hate your job or commute, dislike your boss, or that arrogant co-worker. Give those up!

Over time, you'll learn how to naturally shift your attitudes and heal your mind. Remember, you can't change the past but you can change how you feel about or perceive the past. And that in itself is a powerful way to shift your attitudes, heal your mind, and live Miracle-Minded.

Why lighten your burdens? Forgiveness has benefits. Forgive everything that previously denied you your Ideal Life Path: jobs, careers, relationship conflicts, and your faulty perceptions and decisions. Your forgiveness of ugly past experiences sets you free. Releasing instills in you a sense of inner peace and confidence so you can happily move on without any burdens to slow you down. There are appropriate times to slow down and times to Rock Your World!

You may find solutions to creativity issues while you are still and quiet. While your mind is open and sometimes, when you least expect it, answers will unexpectedly form. It's almost like there's an antenna on the top of your head receiving creative solutions.

Remember that this is Goal-directed Meditation and you may receive guidance that helps you reach your goals. You might want to keep a notebook and pen handy for when that happens. It can be distracting to stop meditating, open your eyes, and write but not remembering an important solution is to me, more distracting. I recommend inviting all valuable guidance, information, and clues to enter your mind before you start.

Health Benefits of Meditation

Health experts, physicians, and long time meditation practitioners extol the virtues of a meditation or Spiritual practice. I personally trained in Mindfulness-based Stress Reduction techniques with medical experts from the University of Boston Medical Center (UMASS). I've discovered both health benefits and Spiritual benefits of meditation, which I've listed below. Those key benefits in themselves are reason enough to take up a healthy stress reduction practice like Mindfulness Meditation ... regardless of your personal goals.

1. Reduced stress and anxiety: Meditation is known to calm the mind and activate the relaxation response, which slows the heart rate, lowers blood pressure, and decreases the production of cortisol, a stress hormone.

2. Improved mental focus and concentration: It's known to be helpful in improving mental focus, concentration, and memory. Meditation enhances cognitive function and attention deficit disorders. Experts also suggest a slowing down of the aging process and a higher level of awareness leading to less falls, mindless wandering, or confusion. This is attributed to staying in the present moment.

3. Immune function: Meditation may boost the immune system by increasing the production of antibodies and improving overall immune function.

4. Reduces symptoms of depression: It can be an effective tool to increase feelings of well-being, happiness, and overall life satisfaction.

5. Meditation lowers blood pressure: Studies found that it can help lower blood pressure in people with hypertension, reducing a risk of heart disease and stroke.

6. Enhances sleep quality: Meditation can help to improve sleep quality and make it easier to fall asleep and stay asleep. You can use the body scan method to prepare for better sleep.

7. Meditation improves emotional well-being: It helps to cultivate a sense of inner peace and emotional stability. It can reduce negative emotion such as anger, fear, and sadness and increase positive emotions.

8. Meditation may also reduce symptoms of chronic pain, such as back pain, headaches, and arthritis.

9. It causes you to slow down. The slowing down process in meditation, starting with your thoughts and breath, will eventually be carried over to your daily life experiences. The value of mindfulness is paramount when you find yourself automatically thinking through your actions and not emotionally overreacting to unpleasant life experiences.

Slowing down your breathing so it's deep and not shallow helps your intentions to become more purposeful. There are times when the body must move quickly but overall, slower movements benefit the body by allowing it to move with intention and not panic. You'll have less physical injuries by becoming more mindful.

Meditation is a powerful tool for promoting mental, Spiritual and physical health. It's a simple practice that can be done anywhere, at any time, and has numerous benefits for both the mind and body. You give a small amount of input for a great amount of output. Whether you find value in meditation for finding your Ideal Life Path, gaining insights for creative projects, or having a stronger relationship with your Higher Power, you'll find your effort is well rewarded.

As a human, you'll always be besieged by some kind of stress or anxiety. Having an inner Resource for inner peace is immeasurable. Improved mental focus and concentration becomes a true gift as one ages. Boosting immune function and lowering blood pressure are truly gifts from the gods.

I once had a management position in a Northern California retirement home and saw first hand the pain and suffering of old age. It's worth it to get a head start. These health benefits may not be so important to you if you're in your twenties or thirties, but a Spiritual practice is like having your good health in a *bank savings account*. You'll notice when your friends and family members have deteriorating health conditions and you enjoy the fruits of your labor by experiencing good health.

*** **Happiness**—A female speaker on a recent webinar said she decided to meditate longer than her standard ten minutes. Her goal was one hour. Her extra effort proved valuable when she miraculously created a new title and a new online course about "Happiness." Creativity often comes at the most unexpected times and unexpected ways.*

Spiritual Benefits Of Meditation

I've recently upgraded my meditation education. According to the current experts there are many more inner benefits beyond having better health. You may acquire more acute intuitive abilities through your attentive or mindful awareness. There is greater receptivity from higher intelligence and the possibility of increased psychic abilities.

I can attest to the validity of these claims through my own experiences with meditation. The most important benefit, for your purpose, is to receive spiritual aid in discovering your Ideal Life Path.

People have practiced yoga and meditation for thousands of years and used them as an alternative form of exercise to keep the mind and body healthy. Scientists recently concluded that a regular meditation and yoga practice can reverse the molecular reactions in your DNA that lead to depression, anxiety, cancer, and other health issues.

*** **Yoga**—A weekend yoga retreat in Northern California healed my aching knees. I didn't do yoga perfectly, but my meager actions were effective and long lasting in healing my chronic knee pain. I've also been successful with CBD oil.

If you haven't started your Spiritual practice yet, this would be a good time to start. You can begin with just ten minutes a day and build up to thirty minutes or more over time. Include your goals and get ready for your life to change. Your future is waiting.

Three Ways to Activate Your Goals

There are three ways to activate your goal-directed Meditations: listen to your own inner thoughts, listen to guidance from your Higher Power, and use Affirmations to activate your next steps. The details are below.

Way #1: Listen to your own self/inner thoughts. The process is important in that firstly, you are initially listening to your own self ... your ego/mental chatter usually speaks first. It may distract you from positive, loving feelings toward yourself and others. That judgmental and false inner voice can and will tell you you're not worthy, not good enough, or other self-deprecating thoughts. It may tell you your goals are too difficult or not right for you. Ego thoughts may also take you in the other direction, which we call arrogance. These arrogant thoughts are equally destructive and prohibitive to reaching your Ideal Life Path. So the first goal is to not listen to negativity. Think of those thoughts as "thought balloons" that you can poke with a pin and they disappear.

It's always a good idea to listen to and note those negative thoughts that are circulating in your head. They might be revealing some things about yourself that either need to be healed, tossed out, or looked at in some fashion. Those thoughts are there for a reason, so it's good to wake up to them and stop them in their tracks if they're destructive.

Mindfulness practitioners just notice them without judgment and let them go, not giving them any power. After a period of time they typically go away. Remember, they're just thoughts, not necessarily reality. Be aware that dangerous, disturbing, and violent thoughts could be handled through therapy.

Or you may heal and transform them into positive thoughts ... and return them into the Universe to be forever loving to the next person who attracts them ... Love Balloons! The Miracle-Minded call our thoughts "our creations ... which we rule." If you want your kingdom to be kind and loving, transform your thoughts to be the positive ones!

Way #2: Listen to Guidance from your Higher Power.

Secondly, when your negative thoughts are no longer selfishly taking up your mental space, your mind will be a clear and open channel. An open mind is available to receive important guidance from your Higher Power. And while you're in the presence of your Higher Power, you may as well turn over any challenges, pain, despair, and suffering. Why keep those feelings when you can simply give them away.

Way #3: Affirmations and Visualizations for Activating Your Dreams or Goals

Metaphysically minded individuals know that, *"All thought creates form on some level."* Author-Marianne Williamson.

Affirmations are powerful and inspiring words when used to connect your desires with your Higher Power. Affirmations or just focusing on your desires while in touch with your emotions is the way to empower form. Self-created affirmations are a means to reprogram your subconscious mind so you may achieve your goals and not lose focus.

Affirmation means to *make a firm intention*. They are powerful statements that your goal is already realized. During a mind-training program, using affirmations creates a future you desire to experience in this now moment. Affirmations are powerful in their purpose to create a better way of life.

An affirmation is a very specific positive statement directed to your subconscious mind that your goal is ready and waiting for you. You'll incorporate affirmations as inner dialogue to replace negative patterns and programs.

A Tool for Your Personal Growth

What goals would you like to activate right now? List them here:

1.
2.
3.

Here are some key steps to take for creating successful affirmations.

Start with a positive statement. You'll want your affirmations to be empowering, so state them in a positive form. Focus on what you want to achieve or experience, not what you don't want. **Example:** *"I don't want to lose my boyfriend."* **Best:** *"I treat my relationships with respect and love so we remain together."* Or *"I communicate in ways that show my love."*

Affirmations are always written in the present tense. *"I am joyful in my new relationship!"*

Affirmations are specific: The more specific your affirmation is, the easier it is to remember, focus on, and manifest. *"I am focused on saving $200 a month for a down payment on an electric car."*

Keep it short and simple. Affirmations should be easy to remember and repeat throughout the day.

Repeat daily: Be consistent with your affirmations. Repeat them as often as you can. You'll reinforce them and make an impact on your subconscious mind.

Have belief and trust: If you don't believe in what you desire, how do you think you'll get it? Focus is key. Remind yourself, "why" your requests are necessary and present your affirmations to your Higher Power to be accepted and manifest. Expressing an emotional connection to your desires gives them energy and impact.

The procedure for writing your own affirmations is to be realistic. Present tense, short and simple is most affective. *" I am peaceful, healthy, strong, and wealthy."* Repeat affirmations throughout your day. They can be used alone or with guided imagery.

More examples:

"I am confident and capable."

"I am surrounded by love and abundance."

"I am healthy and strong."

"I am worthy of success and happiness."

*** **Prime the Pump**—When I was in my mid twenties my parent's purchased a cabin on a five acre plot of land on the Tippecanoe river near Monticello, Indiana. A pump was used to transfer well water into the kitchen and bathroom of their summer cottage. To get the pump to work they had to force water into it to expel air, which began to pressure the water up and out. They called it, "Priming the Pump."*

During the 2020 pandemic, the government stimulated the economy by injecting more money into the system. They primed the pump.

For your purposes priming the pump means putting forth effort, time, and reprogramming to build a solid foundation to get the most benefits out of your Spiritual practice. You are learning how to create affirmations ... positive words and feelings toward your goals. You'll soon learn the "why's" of visualization. Let's Prime the Spiritual Pump!

Prime the Pump by Visualizing Success

Going to your mental and Spiritual well to retrieve something valuable ... water, wellness, or inspiration. Story is an ancient metaphor for going deep within yourself to bring up something you need or desire ... your goal. Keep in mind that the well is your super-conscious mind during your meditations. You want to go very deep to make the Spiritual connection. That's why you must be consistent ... to build on your momentum.

Going to the well is the first step. Keep in mind a goal, such as your Ideal Life Path or creating a closer relationship with your Higher Power. Deep inside are the answers you are looking for! And the answers are often revealed over time as needed. And yet the activating step is priming the pump ... going into the silence. Priming the pump (or pumping the handle) is a way to get the air out of the line so water comes to the surface. It's a metaphor for going deep into the well to discover the thoughts, perceptions, and actions (that come to the surface) to stimulate the Oneness that inspires growth and success.

Consistent visualizations and/or mental rehearsals will prime the pump of your dreams or Ideal Life Path by allowing you to have clarity. You can't achieve anything without clarity first and secondly, a plan to achieve it. Visualizations are known to be a positive step toward achieving your goals. Visualize yourself already having what you desire and feel the emotions associated with receiving your desires.

It's a well-known fact that two of the biggest human fears are public speaking and death. The solutions to these fears are to prepare yourself in advance. If you were giving a speech or presentation before an audience, you would rehearse your words over and over and memorize them until they become second nature to you. You'll notice that successful actors, comedians, coaches, public speakers, and politicians practice their presentations in a mirror before delivering their important messages.

You may also record yourself; your movements, and facial expressions to make sure your body language is congruent with your words. You are priming the pump for a perfect and effective presentation.

The fear of death may also be overcome with greater Spiritual awareness and reading books or watching movies about people who have had near death experiences. They return from their NDE with positive and inspiring experiences.

You'll visualize your steps toward awareness of your Ideal Life Path in the same way. Prepare your affirmations ahead of time, just like a speech, and say them while visualizing yourself in a position of success.

For example, let's say you believe your Ideal Life Path is to become a professional golfer. You've dreamt about it, you've trained, you're an above average golfer, and you see yourself competing professionally and winning competitions.

You would visualize yourself on the golf course, standing on the green with your clubs and bag. You pull the correct golf club from the bag, knowing that the perfect club, your knowledge of the golf course, your physical stance, and the power and accuracy with which you swing the club will get you within the perfect range of each hole.

"I am an expert golfer."

"I consistently make the right and perfect judgments and decisions."

"I am relaxed and in control of my mental state, swing, and the ball."

Try this process with any dream or goal you have. See it in your mind's eye first then transfer that skill into your experience.

Build Inner Strength Through Repetition

The qualities that many people feel they are lacking is the inner strength, confidence, and the courage to take on risks or go after what they want. There are a couple of ways to build inner strength through your meditation practice. Why, you may ask? It's at the level of thought and acceptance that you can build on your inner Resources. Use your mental faculties: bypass your conscious mind to access your subconscious and super-conscious mind through focused and deep quiet time. Listen to what is coming through you: words, images, insight, intuition, and/or a Spiritual download of wisdom or necessary information.

Another way is repetition, just like Tina Turner when she repeatedly chanted. Through chanting, the specific words gave her the courage and strength to stand up to her abusive husband. It works that way with affirmations too or repeating the word "Om" or "One" while sitting in silence.

If you've ever taken the well-known Dale Carnegie Course, you know that repetition beats fear in public speaking and most anything else you want to overcome. The key is to, *"Increase exposure to anything that you fear."*

Repeatedly taking small steps toward the fearful situation helps build confidence in overcoming it! See the thing you fear as something small and inconsequential and see yourself as larger and more powerful. Immersion and repetition equals confidence and freedom!

Three Approaches to Your Goal-directed Practice

There are three ways to approach the process of meditation and goal-directed meditation. In the first generic way, you can *state your own goals approach* in the form of affirmations and visualizations. Do this before and after the meditation. It can be quick and easy if you are focused. I've shown you how to create a successful affirmation in this chapter, and visualizations are sprinkled throughout this coaching program.

The second *surrendering approach* is simpler and easier. The goal is to connect and align with your inner wisdom, with the understanding that your inner wisdom or Higher Power knows exactly what needs to change for you to be happy, peaceful, or knowledgeable. This approach encourages you to surrender what you believe is important in order to discover your Higher Power's will for you.

In a previous chapter; The A.R.T. of Listening I shared how my very first approach (surrender) to meditation led me to overcome a life-threatening situation with drug abuse.

In this approach your Higher Power is allowed to lead you, guide you, and fill in the blanks that are in your own best interests. I've been successful at both approaches and suggest you try them both. Your intuition will let you know the best one at any given time.

The third *mind training approach* is for the Miracle-Minded who study the book *A Course in Miracles*. The non-profit that publishes the book is called The Foundation for Inner Peace. *A Course in Miracles* presents a book on Course theory, and then initially trains its students to affirm its 365 daily lessons ... from 3-5 minutes at a time. You do not sit for hours at a time in meditation. Instead, students state simple affirmations via the Workbook Lessons of the Day. You are guided to repeat them throughout the day, constantly reminding yourself of their efficacy. This ultimately leads to the specific goal of inner peace by shifting your thoughts from *a fear-based thought system to a love-based thought system* ... a miracle!

Each daily lesson becomes part of a meditative journey to bring about a transformative change of mind. This leads you to overcome or overlook the challenges that appear to threaten you. They're just appearances, not reality. This mind training eventually asks students to focus for 10-15 minutes or a bit longer and to repeat the affirmations periodically throughout the day. This provides for consistency and repetition, which are proven practices for positive change.

What is Mindfulness? Mindfulness means bringing your attention to the present moment without judgment. Mindfulness helps to increase your awareness and develop a greater sense of clarity and focus. There are many books written on Mindfulness. One of the most popular is *"The Power of Now"* by author, Eckart Tolle.

The following explanation and components are enough to serve your purpose of getting to a deep level of mind where you hear an inner Voice.

The Five Components of Meditation

There are several components of meditation that are useful in helping you focus inward and nudge yourself towards alignment. You'll focus inward through the rituals of a particular sitting position, your mantra or chanting, and your breath. Together they help you prime your pump. Here they are:

1. Intention: Setting an intention is the same process as creating an affirmation and visualization in Goal-directed Meditation. Intention can help to create a sense of purpose and focus. This can include intentions related to personal growth, stress reduction, cultivating positive emotions, and learning your Ideal Life Path.

2. Non-judgment: Practicing non-judgment and non-expectation is also an important approach to meditation. Accepting whatever thoughts, emotions, or sensations arise during meditation may help to create a sense of peace and non-attachment. Whether your goal is to discover your Ideal Life Path or heal a health issue try your best to not be disappointed if you don't reach your goal right away. Being persistent and consistent can help you establish a powerful habit to create lasting change.

3. Sitting or lying Position: Many meditation teachers invite you to sit in a comfortable and upright position. I'm a believer in being comfortable while meditating. Ask your body what it wants: to sit in a chair, on the floor in a lotus position, or lie down on a yoga mat or bed. People who sit on a chair, cushion, or bench are asked to sit straight with a straight spine, hold your head upright with both feet on the floor.

There's a type of meditation for lying down called Yoga Nidra or "yogic sleep" This type of meditation is ideal for complete relaxation. Relaxation is necessary for a guided journey and going inward to visualize an experience. The idea here is not to fall asleep but to awaken.

4. The Breath: Your breath is the stuff of life. We're told the Christian story of when God breathed life into a handful of dirt and the first spirit, Adam, was made in the image of his Creator. From our first breath to our last, we breath in and out a life force that allows us the freedom to create, love, and learn who we are in truth. That truth sustains us along with the breathe of life.

Deep breathing throughout your meditation practice can help keep your inward focus and proclaim to the Universe, *"I am life!" "I am here to know who I really am." "I am worthy." "I am an innocent child of Spirit." "I am here to align with my Higher Power." "I am here to do my Higher Power's will." "I am here to learn my Life Purpose!"* Or any other words that are important to you.

Continue to breathe deep from your diaphragm, and then shift your focus onto your inner mind. You can use affirmations or surrender into the Universal flow. Stay as long as you are comfortable, no less than five minutes, then slowly come back to conscious awareness. Stretch your body and bask in the experience of connecting with the Divine.

5. Mantra: Words are quite powerful in the meditative realm. Mantras absorb your attention and still the mind. You'll begin with a mantra that raises your energetic vibrations. The word OM or ONE is most commonly used as well as the name of God. If you prefer to chant, simply follow the chanting words you're familiar with.

Ideal Life Path Affirmations

Before going into your next meditation, verbally repeat the positive path-affirming statements below. Remember that you don't know, at this point, what would best drive your life and happiness forward. Surrender what you think you know and turn over your ideas or assumptions to your Higher Power. Let it be okay to start from scratch, have an open mind, and allow your guide/Teacher to fill it with It's own right direction for your peace and happiness.

This affirmation is for you, *"The experience of my Ideal Life Path comes to me easily and effortlessly. I am ready!"*

Here are some examples to use along with the main affirmation:

"I am in tune with what Spirit or the Universe destines me to be, create, or manifest into the world."

"I am a servant of Spirit and I realize the thoughts and perceptions that bring happiness into my life."

"I am ready for change and I now manifest Spirit's will and mine."

*** Rejuvenate—My position at a non-profit in San Rafael, California was located in a semi-rural setting where deer wandered the grounds and ducks swam in the nearby stream. My half hour lunchtime gave me the opportunity to partake in a daily walking meditation on a path by the stream. I returned to work as a new and rested person ready to take on the next project. Is there a quiet place near your workplace where you can go for a short time to reflect, rejuvenate, and restore your inner peace? Go there to rejuvenate yourself.*

Access Your Levels of Mind

In this section you'll learn about brain frequency and how the ability to go deeper in your meditation may help you access your subconscious mind as well as deeper states of consciousness. Going to a deeper level of mind, preferably the theta state, may help you make a Spiritual connection. Consider learning that section so you can use it to gain a higher level of awareness during your daily meditations or Spiritual practice.

Use Brain Frequency to Go Deeper

You might be asking, *"what is brain frequency and why does it matter?"* Understanding brain frequency helps you have an awareness of how deeply a sleep/dream state or meditative state is measured. If you've ever tried the powerful state of hypnosis you know that getting to a deeper state or level of mind is where the affirmations take hold and changes are made. If you don't go deep enough to reach the subconscious mind, you'll most likely not lose weight, stop smoking, release your fears or reach other goals.

It takes a bit of practice before you'll be able to gauge any of the four levels of mind you have achieved: beta, alpha, theta, and delta. It's importance lies in how deep a level of mind you achieve. Going to a desired level helps you accomplish what the goal of this coaching program is all about ... hearing the inner Voice of your Higher Power to guide you to and beyond your Ideal Life Path.

There are four levels of brain frequencies or levels of awareness that you'll experience in your daily life and during your meditation practice or sleep state. Unless you have access to and use a biofeedback machine, you'll have to guess at which frequency you are reaching with your mind. Consistent practice will help you determine your success.

It doesn't work if you mistakenly try to make mental changes in the beta or conscious level of mind. This is because your subconscious is not always in agreement with what you desire. There may be underlying issues in your belief system that need to be resolved before you can make the desired changes. If you are at the beta (fully conscious) level throughout your meditation session, you are probably not influencing your subconscious mind enough, and therefore little or no changes will be made.

The one thing that inhibits your progress is resisting the process or trying to control the process, whether consciously or unconsciously. It's important for you to know, and I'll remind you over and over that this process is about letting go not about forcing it to be your own way.

Beta level—This is the level you operate at on a daily basis. You are supposedly highly alert and focused. This is an ideal level in which to take action in your life. The brain operates at 14 – 30 cycles per second at this frequency. Ninety percent of individuals think and act here.

Alpha level—This is the state where you are mentally and physically relaxed, but still alert. The brain operates at 7 to 14 cycles per second. You may only be partially aware of what is going on around you. This is the ideal level for thinking and analyzing problems, but only 10% of people use this level for thinking. This is the ideal level for creativity and deductive reasoning.

The alpha state allows you to get in touch with life skills that may translate into making better decisions, attaining happier relationships, and achieving greater success in business. It allows you to bring the subconscious to the conscious level and that's why you remember incidents or experiences from many years ago. Some of the known benefits of regularly practicing mental exercises or meditation in order to achieve the alpha state are listed in my Goal-Directed Meditation chapter.

Theta level—This is the state of drowsiness or the twilight state, not the Twilight Zone! (This is also the first stage of sleep). The brain operates at 4 to 7 cycles per second. In this extraordinary realm, you are in a waking dream, and vivid imagery may flash in your mind's eye. Experiencing this state helps you to be receptive to information beyond your normal conscious awareness. Some of the same benefits are experienced here as in the alpha state. You may develop your extrasensory perception skills at this level of mind. According to research, theta brain waves are associated with dreaming, visions, and more contact with the subconscious mind.

Delta level—This is the state where you experience your deepest sleep. Several sources report that certain frequencies in the delta range trigger the release of growth hormones, which are beneficial for healing and regeneration. The brain operates at 4 to 5 cycles per second, the slowest brain wave frequencies.

How will you know what level you are at? It can be a little tricky for a beginner to figure out. What many long time meditation students desire to achieve is a state of "no thought" (no controlled or conscious thought). This state is the very deepest state to achieve. If you feel wide-awake or anxious throughout the meditation or sleep state, very little progress may be made toward your goal.

If you feel like you've gone to a deep mental space and lost yourself or have gone blank in some respects, then you are most likely at the alpha or theta state. If you fall asleep, you will enter a deeper zone in which your affirmations may not take hold.

SUCCESS SKILLS

To develop success skills for meditation, you'll need to schedule time during your day to be still and quiet. You may have to get up early or find a quiet place at your workplace to sit for ten minutes or so. Go to a quiet place in your home while your children are studying or watching television. Or just go outside for a walk and find a park bench. You could even sit in your car for ten minutes. There are many options for escaping from a chaotic day to nurture yourself. You'll return a bit more rested and peaceful.

A Tool for Your Personal Growth

Daily Meditation: Place yourself in a quiet room and turn off all distractions for about twenty minutes. Sit in an upright position in a chair with both feet on the floor. Close your eyes, take several deep breaths.

Do a brief body scan to relax your mind and body. Count down from 10 to 1, finding yourself in a peaceful place of your own choosing (garden, seaside, mountain, meadow, farm).

Notice any thoughts popping up in your mind. Allow them to drift away without engaging them. Do the best you can to sink down to a point of *no thought,* and stay there as long as possible.

Wait for any additional insights. Don't be concerned if you don't reach this state. Keep working on it.

Bring yourself back into the room by counting up from 1 to 10, seeing yourself more awake and more alert as you count higher.

Stretch your body to wake up, and notice how your mind and body feel after the meditation ends. Make a note of anything you experienced: sights, sounds, impressions, images etc.

Your Next Steps

Certain skills are necessary for a successful Mindfulness Meditation practice: concentration, willingness, attitude, a sense of commitment, practice, and perseverance. Remember to start with beginners mind ... that you don't know what you don't know and be open to learning and knowing. Remembering these skills throughout your Spiritual practice will help you stay on course with your Spirit-inspired goals.

Throughout this coaching program I've offered several guided imagery sessions. These guided journeys are designed to introduce you to what is possible when you are open-minded and ready for change. You have journeyed into your heart. You've experienced peace and possibilities. You've met your inner Guide. You've met yourself. You'll soon meet your Ideal Life Path.

Consider taking a local meditation class to learn other various techniques and processes. You may also get value from Dharma talks at a local Buddhist or Mindfulness Meditation Center.

CHAPTER TEN

DREAMS—YOUR SACRED GATEWAY

Dreams are your built-in inner messenger and one of the Sacred Gateways. Your Higher Power or inner Guide uses your dream state to reach you in ways that otherwise might not be possible. As I mentioned earlier it's a state where you might be reprogrammed. Notice when you awaken in the morning and your perceptions on a certain topic have changed.

Dreams are the domain of your subconscious and super-conscious mind. It is my firm belief that your daytime naps, sleep time dreams, and meditations are an important gateway to your transformation state. Be open to the sleep time dreams that are more profound and give you valid information regarding your Ideal Life Path.

You might have a busy daytime schedule and not a lot of down time to think about what your Ideal Life Path might look like. That's why your nighttime dreams could play a large role in revealing Guidance and clues about your past, present, and future. I find that Guidance is usually step-by-step so as not to overwhelm you. It's also very personalized.

The Miracle-Minded know that the mind never sleeps, so talking about the significance of sleep and dreams may seem odd. Your dreams are designed to deliver the important inner messages and images from your subconscious and super-conscious mind while you're in a sleep state of quietness, relaxation, surrender, and openness. Sleep time also helps your body replenish its physical, mental, and emotional energy.

Dreams have fascinated humans for millennia, often seen as windows into the subconscious or messages from a higher realm. For those on a Spiritual path, dreams can hold profound significance and offer guidance, insights, and a deeper understanding of one's inner world. Below is an exploration of dreams and their meanings, particularly from a Spiritual perspective.

Understand Your Dreams

Here are some brief and helpful resources to help you understand the value of dreams.

1. Personal Reflection: Dreams often reflect your subconscious mind, revealing hidden desires, fears, and unresolved issues. They provide a mirror to your inner world, allowing you to gain insights into your emotional and psychological state.

2. Symbolic Language: Dreams speak in a symbolic language. Common symbols, such as water, flying, or particular animals can have universal meanings, but they can also be deeply personal. Understanding these symbols often requires introspection and sometimes guidance from dream dictionaries or Spiritual mentors.

Personal Symbols: Dreams often use symbols unique to the dreamer. A river in one person's dream might represent the flow of life while for another it might signify emotional turbulence.

Some symbols are universal and have common meanings across cultures. For example, water often symbolizes emotions, while flying might represent freedom or spiritual ascension.

Dreams as Spiritual Significance

1. Messages from the Higher Self:

Many spiritual traditions believe that dreams are a Gateway for your higher Self or Divine Guidance to communicate with you. They can serve as a direct line to the Divine or higher Self. These messages can offer wisdom, warnings, or encouragement on your Spiritual journey. Dreams may also offer guidance on Spiritual matters, life decisions, and personal growth.

Some people believe prophetic dreams offer glimpses into the future or provide messages from a Higher Power. They often feel different from regular dreams, carrying a sense of importance and urgency.

Dreams allow you to tap into your unconscious mind, revealing hidden desires, fears, and aspects of yourself you might not be aware of while awake.

Spiritual Lessons are another part of dream interpretation and can present lessons in the form of challenges, conflicts, or journeys, mirroring the Spiritual path's trials and tribulations.

2. Healing and Integration—A Tool for Healing

They may allow you to process and integrate experiences, emotions, and traumas that you might not fully address in your waking life. This process can be transformative and aid in your Spiritual growth. These dreams can offer comfort and healing, addressing emotional wounds or helping to process difficult experiences. In a later chapter I'll share a dream that awoke me to an unpleasant childhood experience and how I reckoned with it

3. Lucid Dreaming:

Practicing lucid dreaming—being aware that you are dreaming while in the dream state. It can be a powerful Spiritual practice. It allows for greater control over the dream narrative, exploration of the subconscious mind, and deeper connection with Spiritual truths. Lucid dreams can be powerful tools for self-discovery and Spiritual exploration.

4. Connecting Dreams with Spiritual Practices

Rituals and Intentions: Before sleep, set an intention to receive guidance or insights through your dreams. Rituals like lighting a candle or saying a prayer can help focus.

Integration: Use the insights gained from dreams in your waking life. They can inform your Spiritual practices, personal growth efforts, and life choices.

5. Mythological and Cultural Perspectives

Ancient Cultures: Many ancient cultures, such as those in Ancient Rome or Greece, viewed dreams as messages from the gods. Temples dedicated to dream incubation, like the Asclepions, were places where people sought healing and Divine messages through dreams.

Indigenous Traditions: Indigenous cultures often see dreams as integral to their Spirituality, using them for guidance, healing, and connecting with ancestors or Spirit Guides.

Practical Steps for Dream Work
1. Dream Journal:

Keeping a dream journal helps to remember and analyze your dreams. Write down your dreams as soon as you wake up, capturing as much detail as possible. Over time, you may notice patterns and recurring symbols.

2. Meditation and Intention Setting:

Meditating before sleep and setting an intention to remember your dreams can enhance dream recall. You can also set specific intentions to receive guidance on certain aspects of your life or Spiritual path.

3. Dream Analysis:

Analyzing your dreams involves looking at the symbols, emotions, and narratives within them. Reflect on what these elements might mean in the context of your current life situation and Spiritual journey. Study common dream symbols and meanings, but also consider your personal associations with the dream content.

4. Seek Guidance:

Dreams can be complex and challenging to interpret. Seeking guidance from a Spiritual mentor, therapist, or dream analyst can provide deeper insights and support.

Common Spiritual Dream Themes

1. Flying: Often represents freedom, transcending limitations, and Spiritual elevation.

2. Water: Symbolizes emotions, intuition, and the subconscious mind. Calm waters may indicate peace, while turbulent waters can signify emotional turmoil.

3. Animals: Different animals carry various symbolic meanings. For example, a snake might represent transformation, while a dove symbolizes peace. I once dreamt of a family dog who passed away years ago.

4. Light: Encountering light or luminous beings in dreams can signify enlightenment, Divine presence, and Spiritual awakening.

5. Sub-personalities: We all have parts of ourselves that have not yet been incorporated into our wholeness. Sub-personalities are often a rebellious part of you and want you to know they're part of you. They're often some kind of critic or judge and initially show up in your dream state. Once in a while I'll become aware of a sub-personality who shows up in my dream. The most recent one was a rather renegade looking young woman who was focused intently on her cell phone. She got my attention.

There's a process that alchemical hypnotherapists use called *Conference Room*. While in a relaxed hypnotic state you can call in your various sub-personalities who may be challenging you and bring them together for healing.

This is often used for weight loss, childhood trauma, or parts of you that resist your goals.

Dreams are a rich resource for you if you're on a Spiritual path, offering guidance, healing, and insight into the deeper aspects of your self. Embracing and exploring your dreams can enhance your personal growth and Spiritual journey. They can lead to a more profound understanding of yourself and your connection to your Higher Power.

Take Your Dreams Seriously

Throughout this program I'll share my personal stories of how powerful and significant dreams led me to my Ideal Life Path. For me, they were two separate things. I'll explain later on how I got to that outcome.

I've studied what happens in our minds when we dream and I believe that there are only two or three types of sleep time dreams that we typically experience. I take sleep time dreams seriously and believe dreams are important windows into your internal, external, and supernatural worlds. They guide you, revealing deeper truths not previously apparent to you. I won't disclose every personal mind blowing dream in this program, but I'll include those that are helpful to the Miracle-Minded ... who are seeking your Ideal Life Path.

*** **Death**—Regular nightmares can be a huge red flag warning! I experienced a couple of years of devastating and murderous nightmares. This happened during a period of time in which navigating employee relationships became stressful. I didn't make the association at the time ... that something at work was literally killing me during my dreams. It took a while to discover what it was.

If you're experiencing nightmares, it's time to start looking at your life or those who are in your life that may be doing harm. The same day I finally fired a troubling employee my nightmares stopped completely, not to return again.•

Dreams: A Gateway to Your Power, Passion, and Purpose!

I'll pinpoint three types of dreams that occur when you sleep. You're going to learn what happens when you dream (at night, during a nap, or sometimes in meditation) and how you can determine the dreams' significance to your Ideal Life Path. I realize that there are many ways to interpret or study dreams and I found this narrowing down to be helpful.

What Dreams are Made From:

1. Stuff from your day: Your average dream is merely stuff from your day that you experienced and has varied significance. It has none-the-less affected your subconscious mind on some level. In this type of dream your subconscious is trying to relate something to you, but it seldom reveals anything major. Recurring dreams require your attention to them. Otherwise, they are most likely not leading you to your Ideal Life Path.

Dreams are largely symbolic and can give you insight into your life by exploring that symbolism. Each symbol is an aspect of you even though the symbol or image doesn't look like you. Without some sort of education, it may be difficult to understand the significance of these dreams, symbols, and what they mean. Studying your symbolic dreams with a hypnotherapist or psychologist can uncover unrealized motivations.

Enhanced creativity is another byproduct of this kind of dream. If you're working on a creative project, you may get special insight or images from your subconscious mind during sleep, while meditating, or when you're in a deep thought session. The key to enhanced creativity is to immerse yourself into the appropriate research, professional training on your topic, focused thought, and periods of relaxed thought. Keep an open mind and like a puzzle, discover where pieces fit together. You can bring your creative potential forward while fully awake. It's called "getting into the zone or flow." I think of the zoneas that sacred and Spiritual mental time when your thoughts are in alignment with your Higher Power and ideas literally come to/through you with less struggle.

2. Premonition:

The second type of dream could be a premonition of the future. I believe these types of dreams are rare, and mostly happen to people who have upgraded their psychic abilities or Spiritual awareness. It's possible to receive a vision of your future ... if it's important to your destiny.

3. Your Spiritual Gateway:

The third type of dream is not a dream, but a Spiritual experience. It's an ideal experience, portal, or gateway to discovering your Ideal Life Path or Big Dream. These are fairly unusual and may be uncommon, except when it's time for you to learn your Ideal Life Path. This profound experience may come to you at night while you're sleeping or sometimes through your meditation practice. These are sacred and unique experiences and may give you some insight to apply to your life or a snapshot of what's to come.

During a nighttime dream/meditation, you may have a metaphysical glimpse, a visual image, or a vision of an otherworldly experience that's connected to your Big Dream or Ideal Life Path.

You may also hear an inner Voice guiding you toward an activity, idea, creativity, or experience. This is helpful if you partake in any kind of creative art. The Spiritual experience might be an assignment or reveal a future occupation, business, way of life, or future event.

Think of this Spiritual Dream as a North Star guiding you to a path you may not have previously considered. I've shared stories of when I was guided to move from Chicago to Northern California, to go on a pilgrimage in Israel, or go to college for graphic design.

When you have this kind of powerful dream experience, your Higher Power wants you to go in a particular direction and believes you have what it takes to get there. This is really an important gift and a more solid foundational experience than a made up fantasy-type dream.

Be aware that you may hear any important Guidance first thing in the morning when you're more likely to remember it and apply it to your life situation.

Tools for Your Personal Growth

Keep a journal notebook next to your bed and write down any dreams that you can remember. Look for any significant symbols, visions, or ideas that give you insight to your current or future life path.

SUCCESS SKILLS

The skill needed to bring about your intuitive success is the self-awareness you're currently building up. It's your focused personal presence during your moment-to-moment life experience that becomes an important skill.

*** **My Day to Die**—I was in my late 30's when I experienced a life-changing dream that awakened me to the potential of a more free and adventurous life. In my dream, I knew it was my day to die, that sometime during that day, I would meet the end of my life. I saw myself then, as I looked in my late-thirties, walking back and forth on a porch, trying to figure out how I would die that day.

I pondered the idea; would a plane crash into the house killing me instantly, or would someone randomly shoot me dead on my porch, or would I have a heart attack as I sat there in the rocking chair?

After a long while and way too much debate, I had to let it go. I got it! It wouldn't be revealed to me in advance. I would just have to wait and see.

That was the end of the dream, but not the end of my response. Soon after the dream ended, I heard myself say in my own voice, *"I wish I had done more with my life."* I wasn't sure at the moment what "more" meant. I assumed it would be up to me. That final thought changed my life for good. I realized it was a Spiritual message to my Self, an insightful gift! From that moment on, I knew that I would not and could not continue to follow the same path, do the same work, or live my life the way I had in the past.

I had to be brave, get out of my own way, and out of my comfort zone. I eventually took the steps to make that happen and have lived my life courageously, not as that once meek teenager growing up in rural Indiana.*

Dreams as an Entryway to Your Future

Aligning with your Higher Power's plan for your life allows you to experience a more joyful, fulfilling, and purposeful life … and that generally means having no regrets. There are many reasons to pursue your Dreams and not wait too long to start taking important steps. Some of the saddest stories about the human experience are when people express their regrets. You've aged or lost your health, and some opportunities are gone forever.

Those are the experiences you could have chosen and didn't, or you chose a specific experience and afterwards wish you hadn't. We all have those experiences. In hindsight you can look back and justify those decisions or explore what you learned. At the end of the day I believe most of us would rather not have those regrets.

*** **My Day to Die Follow-up**—My 'end-of-life' dream experience was a powerful gift to me. It set me free from a career and life that had run its course. I could no longer spread my wings or have the adventure my soul craved. For my emotional well-being, I understood that I needed to face the truth and move on. To me, that brief dream was every bit as important as the inevitable unfolding of my Life Purpose, Dream, and Vision. I looked at every aspect of my life differently from that point on.

Life is a precious experience and to not honor and celebrate it to the fullest is to not appreciate what Spirit has in store for you. You should not get to the end of your life knowing it could've been amazing!*

How to Handle Regret

Sooner or later, you may have feelings of regret for something you've done or said in the past. Of equal regret may be what you haven't said or done in your past. The Miracle-Minded let go of the past. No matter what you see in movies or on television, it's fiction, and you can't change the past. But you can move forward more mindfully, remembering that you can forgive yourself, let it go, and choose differently next time. If you are fortunate to have a life-changing dream like mine, I suggest you take it to heart. Otherwise:

1. You can either change your life, situation, or circumstances like I did and remedy the (potential) regret before it occurs or it's too late.

2. You can let it go for another day when you're motivated to make a life change.

3. You can let it go completely and find peace and fulfillment in whatever you've chosen.

Your Life Path is Not Always in a Direct Line!

The path to your ideal occupation/Dream and massive happiness is not always a direct line from A to B. From all the people I interviewed for this coaching program, you'll most likely take a zigzag journey ... similar to a maze.

Think of the Crooked Street in San Francisco. It zig zags back and forth a number of times, but still gets you to the bottom of Lombard Street where you look back at the journey and the environment and say, *"Wow!"*

You don't have to have a profound dream that points out to you that life is (relatively) short. Your Higher Power is guiding you every step of the way, whether you see it happening or not. Think through what you want out of your life. If you feel strongly about something, include it in your goals or life plan. Remember, you're Miracle-Minded.

Although you'll see from my story that I was not only open to living a freestyle life, but my Higher Power guided me right along and used my adventurous spirit to bring me a more interesting life. I've be sent where I could be truly helpful and will put you where you'll be truly helpful to those who need you and your wisdom, gifts, and talents!

There's a popular saying, *"Life doesn't happen to you, it happens for you!"* Let this quote sink in and help you to reframe the situations that appear to be a struggle for you.

Joseph Campbell, the well-known author and mythologist who introduced the concept of "The Hero's Journey" said, *"Follow your bliss and doors will be* *open to you where there were not doors before."* Another way of saying that is to *follow your passion.* I've pointed out in earlier stories that passion doesn't work out for everyone. Your feelings of passion might be confused with infatuation, which is a temporary, less meaningful level of passion/bliss! Search your soul to determine if your Dream is a passion, an infatuation, or a meaningless distraction.

How will you know you're on the right track? There will be signs, synchronicities, and serious ooh's and aah's! Doors will open and you'll step through them with ease.

You'll ask yourself, *"How did that mysteriously happen?"* It's like saying the magic word or waving your magic wand. The Universe responded to your thoughts and actions, and it doesn't get any better than that. Just take the next step. Did a door open? Yes or no? Then take the next step and the next and keep moving forward. It takes a lot of trust to live this way, but it's awesomely better than being held back by fear, struggle, or a limited belief in yourself.

Trust in the Process

Whether it's the Gateway of sleep time dreams or your meditation practice ... trust in the process. The words or images you experience are significant road signs to your destination. What are they saying to you or leading you toward? Against all odds and when the time is right, you'll move forward by acting on your intuition. Intuition is going inward to receive insight. It leads you to take small steps and ultimately you'll reach your destination/ destiny.

The challenge is that after a number of years, you might have a family, a mortgage, and other obligations that may hinder your search for your Dreams or an Ideal Life Path. Instead, you pursue a money making career because you're required to care for a family. Seeking for your Big Dream may seem frivolous to your mate, friends, and family. Again, don't let that stop you from some serious inquiry. Life can rapidly change and new opportunities or open doors can show up at your doorstep.

You and your family may find it advantageous to make a shift together! If you have a Dream, talk about it to those you love who are part of your life. Give them a chance to support you and help you get to where you need to be. Turn your concerns over to your Higher Power so you can get a new perspective or directions. You can't do this alone, nor should you have to. You have a Divine partner, so take advantage of that resource.

Be open-minded about what you can learn about yourself and new possibilities available to you. You don't have to change your life right this minute. Be open to how, over time, your life may change in subtle ways. Once you step forward, your Ideal Life Path starts to unfold before you.

Here's how it might unfold for you:

1 You have high hopes that you'll reach your Spirit-inspired goals quickly.

2. You become disenchanted when point A and point B are far apart in time.

3. You have some missteps and there are detours, but you learn valuable life lessons.

4. You then go on another search for a career that suits you or is easier to attain. It can turn out to be a cycle of mismatched careers and disappointments. You start over again and again. If that happens to you, don't lose faith.

"Be persistent toward what you believe to be your Ideal Life Path."

5. The Miracle-Minded don't give up! You'll say to yourself, *"I'm frustrated, so how do I learn of my Ideal Life Path? Oh, yeah, I was told to align my thoughts and perceptions to my Higher Power first!"*

Your Next Steps

Your sleep time dreams are truly the gateway to your Ideal Life Path. Write in your journal anything that stands out to you. I believe you'll experience a quickening of dreams when it's time to step into your Ideal Life Path. In coming chapters you'll learn from my personal stories how night time dreams led me across the country where I could access the skills I needed to do my Higher Power's will.

In the next chapter you'll learn about another gateway to your Ideal Life Path where you'll find yourself connecting with your Higher Power on a deep level of mind.

CHAPTER ELEVEN

ALIGN WITH YOUR HIGHER POWER

"Worry is the most useless emotion!" **Linda L. Chappo**

Are you consumed with worry about your future? If so, you may be misaligned in your relationship with your Higher Power. Do you wonder what's next for you? Are you spinning your wheels, going from job to job or career not really growing or accomplishing your Dreams? You know you have potential, but are not getting a chance to use it? All of these questions and concerns mean you aren't aligned with your Higher Power and Its plan or will for your life. Hopefully, that's the first thing on your mind.

I've included a helpful prayer from the Workbook Lessons in ACIM to help guide you in your efforts. It's in this chapter under: A Tool For Your Personal Growth.

Do you fear that tuning into your Higher Power for your important decisions won't propel your career and life forward? The Miracle-Minded know that your *detour into fear* can keep you stuck where you are if you allow it! Aligning your belief system with love and trust, not fear, can change everything for good in ways that forcing it never will.

WHY IS THIS IMPORTANT?

You'll learn that everything in alignment with your Higher Power is destined to happen. But what if, after all these questions, exercises, and Tools for Personal Growth … you're still not sure what's in alignment?

Have you read the previous chapters, the Success Skills, and used the Tools for Your Personal Growth? Are you practicing the *A.R.T. of Listening and Goal-directed Meditation?* These tools are designed to help you build a Spiritual Foundation so you can be in alignment with your Higher Power.

Continue to immerse yourself in the material because in the chapter, *The Process of Discovery*, you'll take a higher level of exploration into the deeper parts of your human experience. Remember, this coaching program is for readers who are serious about learning their Ideal Life Path and getting off life's roller coaster.

Begin to Align with Spirit

The only real problem that you have, according to ACIM, comes from your seeming separation from your Higher Power. Do you feel separate or think thoughts of separation? Separation thoughts go something like this: *"I don't feel my Higher Power's presence in my life"* or *"I don't get a sense that my Higher Power is listening to me or helping me in any way."* Those thoughts of a separated mind means you're out of alignment or you're absent-minded. You've forgotten who you are!

Healing the separation through *the act of conscious connection* will open up the road ahead. You'll learn how to do that with the Tools for Personal Growth. *Asking through prayer, listening through meditation, and exhibiting kindness to all are three of the best ways to bring your Higher Power into focus.* There are times to be active, passive, or patient.

Here are some thoughts on what being in alignment might look like. The Miracle-Minded self-identify as a Spirit having a human experience. You stay away from judging others. You shift from a fear-based thought system to a love-based thought system. You know you are not a victim. You keep forgiving yourself and others knowing that innocence is your true nature. You keep God/Higher Power as first in your life. You have the awareness that the Kingdom of Heaven is at hand, and you offer everything that would hurt you over to your Higher Power. If you've studied other metaphysical teachings, these ideas from ACIM are fairly similar. Remember that you, as Spirit, are made in His image.

As your parents love and care for you, they direct you to everything that is good for you. So does your Higher Power! Does it make sense to you that your Higher Power would direct you to your heart's desire? If so, trust that your aligned subconscious and super-conscious mind will support you in your efforts. Think about it! If your actions don't manifest your desires, maybe your desires are not the right fit for you in this moment? Remember that your life is lining up for you in your Higher Power's time, not yours. Yes, that was a difficult pill for me to swallow. So what did I do?

*** Follow Your Guidance—I lived my life the best I could by following my Spiritual guidance the best I knew how. There were times I received no guidance that I was aware of. I still worked toward my various personal goals, enjoyed my vacations, had fun with friends and romantic partners, and basically enjoyed my life. These enjoyments are also in your Higher Power's plan for you. Why wouldn't they be? *To be Spiritual is to be who you are.

Remember that your Higher Power is not a tyrant and only wants you to be happy. So, you must allow Him to accomplish that by not only turning over your problems, but turning over your decisions to One who knows what's in your own best interests.

I attended a lecture by the popular and insightful personal growth expert and author Sonia Choquette. She said, *"The Universe always answers, 'yes!'"* So go ahead and ask for guidance on your ideas. Make plans, take steps, believe in yourself, and trust that you'll be shown the way to that goal or maybe something better ... your Ideal Life Path. Taking action is key. If your action is wrong, you'll know it. Doors will not open for you. Whenever doors open, you know you're on the right path. If one door doesn't exist, ask for another way. As you travel this path road signs will appear, and you'll go to sleep at night knowing that you're headed in the right direction.*

The Road Ahead with Your Higher Power

Detours and bumps in the road are normal and you'll see them for what they are ... valuable learning experiences to remember when you run across a challenge in your life. I've been down this road and I'll share my stories of alignment and misalignment so you're aware of what you might experience. I shared how my Higher Power led me to my college major and its valuable skills. I also shared how that worked out for me after attending part time classes for five plus years. It could have turned out to be a waste of time, effort, and money, but it wasn't. It was the best decision ever!

So, where does alignment happen? It's not always in the church, temple, or mosque of your choice, although it can happen there. It's not necessarily on a pilgrimage or sacred voyage, yet it's possible to have an enlightened experience wherever you go and whatever you do ... even in the most unlikely places. There are no limitations when your Higher Power is involved.

As I mentioned earlier in this chapter, alignment comes from healing the separation and choosing unity instead. The Miracle-Minded know it's at the level of mind that you make your choices and decisions. Having this basic knowledge gives you a better understanding of where your alignment comes from ... a Spiritual connection that begins to groom you for your Ideal Life Path. You'll speed things up for yourself by getting into alignment first.

The grooming process happens over time. You might have a dream that guides you to do something in particular and that causes you to make a different decision. That could be step one. You eventually take a class or meet someone important to your path. That's step two and three. You might take on a job in a specific career. That's step four. And it goes on from there ... following your Guidance or intuition.

Because Spiritual alignment is entirely personal and intimate, you'll have that experience when your Higher Power determines you're mentally, emotionally, and Spiritually ready for a start or a road sign.

Use this information to assure yourself that any time you spend on conscious alignment or connection, mental imagining, or mental rehearsal is time well spent. You'll prepare to have the often subtle experiences that move you toward your Ideal Life Path.

Alignment Through Awakening

How do you awaken and align to who you really are ... a Spiritual being? Different Spiritual teachers will offer their own ways, dependent upon their personal experiences. Here is my suggestion. Depending on your personal belief system, you might read and integrate various religious teachings or other Spiritual texts: Buddhist studies, *A Course in Miracles,* metaphysical teachings like the Unity Movement or the Center for Spiritual Living ... or many prominent personal growth teachers. You could take a class in Comparative Religions to see what resonates with you. I studied a number of Spiritual paths before I discovered the profound self-study training of *A Course in Miracles.*

A serious study of the material told me I was already naturally in alignment with its teaching. It was perfect for me, but it isn't for everyone. I wanted a Spiritual path that didn't claim to be the "only one" or wasn't "all-inclusive." Continue to seek until you find the best one for you.

An inner awakening or Spiritual Rebirth isn't easy to describe because it's a personal experience and is different for everyone. I would call it an expanded awareness of your existence as a free Spiritual being connected to your Higher Power. You'll have an astute awareness that you are not an ego mind trapped in a body with physical, mental, Spiritual, and emotional limitations. You are so much more!

*** **Beginnings**—My childhood consisted of many different religious studies and explorations. My young adult life was spent exploring various Spiritual paths and metaphysics. In my mid forties I was guided in a dream to up the ante. So I spent a great deal of time catching up, so intensely that it led me to a tumultuous breakdown in values. And that included a more profound inner experience of Light, Love, and Emergence as a more enlightened, goal-oriented Spirit/human.*

Your Spiritual Path Must Speak to & Resonate with You!

If your religion, Spiritual path, or metaphysical teaching doesn't speak to you, resonate with your heart, or give you the information or experiences you are seeking, it might be time to search for another path. When you experience an awakening, either in a moment or over a period of time, you'll know it's authentic and real. To align with your Higher Power's will for you is to ask for it, receive the knowledge given, and move forward as you are given guidance.

1. Think the way your Higher Power thinks or *"what would God be thinking that I'm not thinking?"* You might believe this is a difficult thing to do, and if you're practical and come from your heart, you'll automatically know how your Higher Power thinks ... devoid of any ego dum thinking. Your Higher Power thinks with benevolence: honesty, purpose, kindness, wisdom, and love.

2. Live without fear and be brave about what you're guided towards.

3. Pay attention to your thoughts and perceptions. How are they leading you in a new or different direction? How are they encouraging you to be authentic and/or heal specific relationships?

4. If you want to be successful at aligning with your Higher Power, reread the Success Skills and learn to use them wherever and whenever you can.

*** **Am I kind enough?**—It's possible to randomly tap into your subconscious or super-conscious mind. As I sat at my computer one afternoon I slipped into a light trance. You might think of it as zoning out or daydreaming, which we all do from time to time. During that brief time I established an alignment and a surprising personal connection and internal dialogue with my Higher Power.

Spirit and I had an unusual conversation about *how kind of a person I was?* It actually turned out to be a debate about *"If I was as kind a person as I thought I was?"* At first I was a bit insulted at this topic. I insisted that I was a kind person and shared a few examples of how kind I am to family, friends, and people I know.

After some conversation, I agreed that there had been numerous times in my past where I was selfish, unkind, perhaps mean-spirited, or thoughtless toward others. Of course, I regret those behaviors and pray they stay in the past. And yes, I finally determined that I could be kinder to people I didn't know. I was asked if I could *"take it up a notch?"* Of course, I agreed that I could and would do that.

So from that point on I've done my best to be kinder to people I interact with every day: store clerks, waiters, service people, sales people, and whoever crosses my path throughout the day. I would acknowledge them by smiling more often, being friendly, and/or asking their name.

According to Dale Carnegie, author of *"How to Win Friends and Influence People"*, he says, *"A person's name is to that person the sweetest and most important sound in any language."* It's so important that I've learned to ask a person's name in various languages when I travel outside of the U.S.A.

Because of this interaction, I learned to be kinder and shine my light a little brighter every day. I would do my part to return the world to the Paradise it was created to be.*

"GOD Does Not Play Dice with the Universe ..." Albert Einstein, Scientist

Go With The Flow

Go with the flow by aligning your thoughts and motivations with your Creator. Get started with co-creating the life you're meant to live, not the one that is too easy, too difficult, or not a match for your Soul! Trying to get your Ideal Life Path under your total control by yourself is a complete waste of your time and energy. Be open to learning what your Higher Power has in store for you, go with the flow, and enjoy the journey.

*** **No Accidents**—James lived his life with a major misperception. James, a pleasant and professional young man in his mid to late twenties, came to my home to sell me insurance. We had a conversation that meandered somewhat, and he mentioned in passing that, *"he was an accident."* He didn't show any emotion toward that statement, but it was a red flag for me. I felt a need to address his comment, as it's not a statement of high self-worth to feel unwanted by your parents.

I said to him, *"You mentioned that you were an accident and I question that statement because I've learned that no one is here by accident!"* I continued to share important facts. *"Albert Einstein, the famous Scientist and Philosopher, said, "God does not play dice with the Universe."* In other words, you are not here at random. I continued, *"With all due respect to your parents ... you may have been unplanned in their minds and that doesn't mean you are an accident! In God's plan you're meant to be here and you're here for a reason and a purpose. Your Higher Power's perfect love is extended to you also."*

In ACIM, the Spiritual teaching, Jesus says, *"Remember that no one is where he is by accident, and chance plays no part in God's plan. Be not afraid."* (ACIM M-9.1)

James was quiet after I made my point. I could see he was giving my perspective some thought. I hoped that I helped him to have a more accurate understanding of Spiritual law and that he was designed to be here by the most powerful and loving energy in the Universe.*

* I sincerely hope this attitude is just a generational glitch. *"Parents, never say to your children that they were an accident, even if you believe it."* They were NOT! They were unplanned in your mind but not in the grace of your Higher Power. It hurts a persons' self-esteem to hear their parent say they were unwanted for any reason. All children are a gift or blessing to the world.

Do You Have Free Will or Not —The Script is Written

Have you ever wondered if everything in life is predetermined? As I talk with various Spiritually aligned experts, people can't seem to agree on whether we have free will or our lives are predetermined. I'll dip into that topic in this section and you can juggle it around in your own mind.

Dreams or fantasies can change over the years. You may have achieved one of your Dreams and are ready for another. You may tell yourself that your last Dream wasn't your real purpose. If that's true for you, it's time to go right to your Source/Higher Power and align your thoughts, perceptions, and actions with His ... not with any ego-dum fantasies.

Do you know if your Higher Power is on board with your Dreams or fantasies? Were you guided to take certain steps? If not, what did you learn? Having an over-controlling personality is often detrimental to your success. Did you fail? I had several failures from doing my own thing. The Miracle-Minded know that, *"The script is written."* (ACIM W-158)

Are you uncertain if you're receiving guidance? You can take the reigns, but miraculous breakthroughs or open doors may or may not occur for you.

The Miracle-Minded can learn a lot about the mechanics of the world from Albert Einstein and also from ACIM. One of Albert Einstein's most famous quotes is, *"God does not play dice with the Universe."*

The Encyclopedia Britannica, referring to physicist Albert Einstein: *"He is also firmly determinist. As far as Einstein was concerned, God's 'lawful harmony' is established throughout the cosmos by strict adherence to the physical principles of cause and effect." "Thus, there is no room in Einstein's philosophy for free will."*

Einstein said, *"Everything is determined, the beginning as well as the end, by forces over which we have no control ... we all dance to a mysterious tune, intoned in the distance by an invisible player."*

The Ultimate Plan

ACIM says the same things, but in a different way. It says, *"... yet there is a plan behind appearances that does not change. The script is written."* (ACIM W-158) So, no matter how life appears on the surface, there's a higher plan going on underneath your experience in the world. You have relatively little idea why certain things happen, whether they are good, bad, or ugly! Another ACIM workbook lesson says, *"Only God's plan for salvation will work."* (ACIM: W-71) Salvation can be interpreted as happiness!

Here is a quote from ACIM that I believe is totally comforting: *"What could you not accept, if you but knew that everything that happens, all events, past, present, and to come, are gently planned by One Whose only purpose is your good?"* – (ACIM: W-135)

And yet ACIM also says that your plan and your Higher Power's plan is the same, so it appears as if you're partaking in the plan whether you're consciously aware of it or not. That's good news if you're attuned to your Higher Power's plan for your life.

So I understand that to mean 'you are birthed with the sacred seed of who you are to become and you'll be led, guided, influenced ... whatever, along certain paths. When the time is right, you'll make a shift or a different decision. Otherwise, you'll do whatever personally brings you a sense of purpose, peace, and happiness.

What I'm attempting to say here is that, *"you can't do it wrong!"* While it may not look or feel right to you in this moment, you're working through some things ... karma or whatever. You'll eventually get into a place that's in alignment with your Higher Power and even with another person or persons.

There might be a delay or a glitch in that holistic health center, yoga studio, hypnotherapy practice, church, Spiritual retreat center or business you want to buy or start from scratch. Let it be okay for now ... until the Universe brings the right people or elements together.

That person who is right for you might be married to someone else right now, in the military, living in another country, or going through their own tough times. You'll be brought together in the right and perfect time. Trust the plan. Fear not!

*** **Children on a Ride**—I taught my Miracle-Minded students this explanation about free will. Picture the children who have a safe, designated playground at an amusement park. They climb into a little boat that goes around in circles. They have the option of steering it back and forth against the side of the container, but it goes in the direction and at the speed designed by the ride operator.

There are child size helicopters that children can steer to make the ride go up or down. The ride operator determines the direction and a safe speed.

When you're a bit older, you get to drive the bumper cars. Your speed is limited by the car's functions. You'll drive in the direction you desire and bump into other cars but you're limited by the size of the track.

It's the same way with free will. You have a certain amount of leeway, but at some predetermined point you'll be subtly led to your Higher Power's plan for you. I believe this is how it works with free will. You are free to make some decisions and there may be leeway in timing, but *the script is written.**

*** **Free Will?**—An Oct. 6, 2023 article and interview in the New York Times, Robert Sapolsky, a biologist and neuroscientist at Stanford University and recipient of the MacArthur Foundation "genius" grant says he doesn't believe in free will. In his book, *"Determined: A Science of Life Without Free Will."* He contends that we are not free agents, but that biology, hormones, childhood, and life circumstances coalesce to produce actions that we merely feel were ours to choose.*

In the article, Sapolsky does not specifically attribute our thoughts, behaviors, and actions to Spiritual awareness but to one's past. The book can give you more specific information on his unique perspective.

Determinism and Free Will

Let's dip into this question a little deeper. You might be asking, *"If only God's plan for my salvation will work, where does my free will fit in? Do I even have it?"* Many people believe in determinism, like Albert Einstein. You may believe you can choose your life journey on your own, regardless of your Higher Power's plan. There's a passage in the New Testament. In Romans 8:28–30, Paul refers to predestination: *"We know that in everything God works for good with those who love him who are called according to his purpose."*

The astrophysicist, author, and science communicator, Neil deGrasse Tyson says, *"You have the illusion of free will, but in fact, that illusion comes about because you don't know the future. Because you are a prisoner of the present, forever locked in transition, between the past and the future."*

One question I'm asked is, *"Do I have to consciously align with my Higher Power?"* It shows commitment if you do it in a conscious way. Be cautious that your ego might misdirect you. That's what happened to me when I started a business without guidance to do so. I wasn't successful. "When you continue to try to control everything you miss out on the delightful surprises and unexpected gifts from your Higher Power." You also miss out on the miracle i.e. the shift in perception that allows you your personal growth experience.

* **Here's the key:** You'll be given the thoughts and perceptions to align with the plan … if you're listening and not judging or controlling. The good news is that you will get there … in alignment through a change of attitude without forcing it. It will seem as natural as streaming pure water … going with the flow.

SUCCESS SKILLS

Whether you've already discovered your Ideal Life Path or not, know that your patience, confidence, and trust are virtues/skills that hold your place/career Dreams in the larger plan.

Tools for Your Personal Growth

Tool #1: Review your thoughts regarding your Higher Power's plan for you.

Tool #2: ACIM prayer: I Give My Life To God To Guide Today

"Father, I give You all my thoughts today. I would have none of mine. In place of them, give me Your Own. I give You all my acts as well, that I may do Your Will instead of seeking goals which cannot be obtained, and wasting time in vain imaginings. Today I come to You. I will step back and merely follow You. Be You the Guide, and I the follower who questions not the wisdom of the Infinite, nor Love whose tenderness I cannot comprehend, but which is yet Your perfect gift to me." Today we have one Guide to lead us on. And as we walk together, we will give this day to Him with no reserve at all. This is His day. And so it is a day of countless gifts and mercies unto us. (W-233)

Your Part is Important!

Your Higher Power has a plan for your happiness and it affects the resulting happiness of the world. Yes, it's that important! Your part is that you learn to listen inwardly, take direction, and then show up the best you can. Follow your guidance with a willing mind and heart. You won't be left out in the wilderness. You are not alone.

Unlearning Is As Important As Learning

In order to align with your Higher Power and achieve your Ideal Life Path, you may need to unlearn what you thought brought you success or happiness in the past. To create a more enlightened future and get a sense of certainty the Miracle-Minded relearn, acquire, and implement new thoughts, perceptions, and systems. This means looking for answers within you, not outside of you.

In other words go within and ask your inner Guide or inner Teacher first, not after you've explored other options. If you don't hear your inner Voice: sit in silence, be patient, then trust your intuition.

Achieving your Dreams or Ideal Life Path will not rely on past learning. Like a buffet, take from the past what is valuable and leave the rest. We've all heard the quote, *"If you do what you've always done, you'll get what you always got!"* You don't want that. Use your past as a learning experience, but don't dwell there. You want to birth something new ... a new you, one that's Miracle-Minded and wants to make a difference either in your life, your family's life, or in your world! Leave your past pain and despair in the past where it belongs!

You've been trained from birth to live and learn in a way that authorities or educators believe is the most productive to the whole. That's no longer valid! Any intuitive insight, creativity, and Spiritual knowledge that you're born with is overcome by the demands of the subjects you're taught and the competitive nature of the world.

Those ways of living or surviving are somewhat necessary to navigate the current consciousness of the world. The problem is they're devoid of compassion or kindness toward others who are unlike the authority or who are inward leaning.

"Each place along the way is somewhere you had to be in order to be here." - Wayne Dyer, Author, Public Speaker

*** **Row Your Boat**—"Row, Row, Row Your Boat Gently Down the Stream, Merrily, Merrily, Merrily, Life is But a Dream." A simple children's song can be a gentle message for living life simply and happily. It means, 'be gentle, go with the flow, don't work too hard, and be happy every day because life really is a dream.'*

SUCCESS SKILLS

One of the most helpful skills in this chapter, Align With Your Higher Power, is letting go! Let go and allow your Creator to lead you to everything that is meant for you. Don't fight it. There are circumstances that may not allow you to fulfill every detail of your Dreams as you define them. Just know and trust that everything for your good is already arranged for you. No need to worry!

Your Next Steps

After reading this chapter about aligning with your Higher Power, you most likely got my message that everything is planned for your good. So, my point is that your life runs more smoothly and painlessly when you turn over everything to this important relationship. Ease and freedom are yours.

CHAPTER TWELVE

CO-CREATE YOUR IDEAL LIFE PATH

Co-creating something as important as your Ideal Life Path means you'll take an active part with knowledgeable and willing partners ... your Higher Power and Divine helpers. To be clear there are times when you'll be active and other times being passive is the right thing to do. Clear co-creation with your Higher Power leads to the manifestation process that may transform your life and the lives of others. Both large and small steps are necessary to reach your Higher Power's will for you.

That's why it's so important to learn your Ideal Life Path and eventually become a creative channel for wherever your gifts can be of service. Positive change doesn't happen on Earth unless aware and awakened humans like you co-create a goal and take action! You are also your Higher Power's representative or partner on Earth and you have a part in the overall plan. The Miracle-Minded tap into the ways they can be of service and your Dreams or Ideal Life Path are part of the Divine plan.

WHY IS THIS IMPORTANT?

Two or more co-creators come together to create something new, innovative, or unique. The co-creator known as your Higher Power and/or your inner Teacher/Guide is assigned to you to direct you according to Higher Power's will. You are the co-creator who manifests His will into the world. The power of two is immense.

If you don't know this information, now is the time! The first goal to co-creating your Higher Power's will is to focus your energy. Discover your inner Teacher, the one who will personally guide you and speak to you. You may or may not be aware of the Holy Spirit, Angels, Guides, or inner Teachers who may also guide your life in a positive direction.

The Miracle-Minded generally call their Guide/Inner Teacher the Holy Spirit. Beliefs about inner Guides and their names can be a cultural or metaphysical preference. Go with whatever you're comfortable with or your personal experience.

Your inner Teacher takes into consideration who you are, your gifts, and what you're capable of accomplishing. On the other hand I've read stories about totally incompetent people who are guided to accomplish phenomenal things. I'm always inspired by these stories that prove everyone is capable of greatness. Keep in mind you are also endowed with the gifts of God.

You who are psychic, clairvoyant, or clairaudient are most aware of your inner Voice. Your inner Teacher knows why you're here and do their best to relate sacred information to you so you can achieve what you're meant to do, be, or learn. That's why it's important to prepare yourself for listening.

Your connection to what may be called Higher Power's team of helpers is through your mental faculties: your thoughts or what we call the Universal Mind that everyone is connected to! You learned how to listen in the chapter, The A.R.T. of Listening and through your meditation practice. As a reminder, A.R.T. is Activate, Receive, and Trust. Most importantly, remember that you're a co-creator. You don't work alone.

Can you visually see your Guide or inner Teacher? Some people do and others don't, depending on their confidence level or if they feel threatened by an inner Guide's presence.

*** **Guides**—Early in my Spiritual journey I followed the lead of my former Spiritual advisor to learn of my inner Guide. (Shakti Gawain, author of Creative Visualization). I asked her suggested questions before bedtime and my inner Guide revealed himself to me as I awoke the next morning. There was no conversation, just a name and a face. Sometimes your inner Guide will change, depending on your situation. I've come to meet a dark skinned female Guide in several dreams who offered to help me with my creative endeavors.*

Some individuals report conversations with their inner Guides. Gary Renard, a popular *A Course in Miracles* speaker and author of *The Disappearance of the Universe* relates his experiences with Ascended Masters who assist him with his teachings and books. This may be an uncommon phenomenon but his teachings are popular and he helps many Miracle-Minded students.

If you ask, it's possible that your inner Teacher may reveal him or herself to you. Whether you meet an inner Teacher or not, guidance is always given at the super-conscious level, whether you're aware of it or not. I offer a personal growth tool for you to meet your inner Teacher/Guide in Chapter Twelve. This tool could be important in learning who is guiding you on your journey.

Three Reasons You Don't Take Action on Your Dreams

1. You have a fear of failure or you can't see yourself as successful.

2. You don't really believe in your Ideal Life Path or yourself. You may have low self esteem or be averse to risk.

3. There may be a lack of financial support regarding starting a business, or where you need to be creative with financing. There is also a fear of losing money or being unsuccessful after taking out loans.

As you've read, fear is the real reason people don't achieve their Dreams or Ideal Life Path. Ask yourself if there are ways to overcome any of these three fearful reasons that might apply to you? And if you can't, don't, or won't find a promising solution, then make success a goal. Take your questions or concerns to your Higher Power in your meditations.

"How can I see myself successful in learning my Ideal Life Path?"
"What actions must I take?"

"How can I believe in myself more powerfully?"

"What must I do to enlarge my mindset?"

"What resources may I tap into to get a start on my Ideal Life Path?"

"How may I engage more fully with my Higher Power?"

F.E.A.R. stands for False Evidence Appearing Real. Don't let the appearance of what isn't true or real keep you from expressing your creativity, achieving your destiny, or living a happy life. Even if you have to take small steps, be willing to do what you can.

Keep Your Focus and Attention

Keep your focus and put your attention on your desired outcome: happiness in whatever form it takes for you, doing your Higher Power's will or learning of your purpose. To co-create with your Higher Power you may have to push yourself out of your comfort zone and take small steps toward your desires. Achievement often calls for bravado!

What I Know For Sure!

You too may have experienced these situations:

Your Higher Power has it's own ways of helping you to achieve what is meant to be i.e. your destiny. Important thoughts and perceptions come through the unseen Spirit realm to your conscious or super-conscious mind. Your intuition is similar to an invisible antenna that attracts those thoughts or ideas. Double check to make sure they're not ego thoughts.

Your inspired thoughts, which you can think of as synchronistic, will make sense to you, and seem appropriate. They'll lead you to the people, places, and things that are important to your Spiritual unfolding or evolution.

Your Higher Power often brings people together in pairs to achieve goals together. And just like the story of Noah's Ark, you go together two by two or two of a kind. Higher Power is a Universal partner to both of you.

Typically one of you is the others' personal support system. It could be a friend, family member, or co-worker whose role is to lead, support, or nurture you. Or you might be the main support person. Both of you will come together due to your individual gifts: skills, connections, finances, or personal power that are needed to balance out your requirements. Together, each with your inner Guide, you four become unstoppable!

It Takes Two—You are Not Alone!

My goal in this chapter is to drive home the point that you are not alone here or a victim in a threatening world, even if it occasionally appears that way and some of your experiences may affirm that. Believing those lies makes the illusion (that you are separate and unloved) real.

Miracle-Minded individuals with a strong Spiritual practice experience guidance and experiences beyond your normal realm. Many of those experiences will be explored in the stories I share. We have benevolent inner support when we are open-minded or Miracle-Minded enough to hear what is coming to us, through us, and for us! Focusing inward is the new frontier in evolutionary change.

Mind expansion is a wide-open field for those who pursue it and want to learn how the brain and mind have different functions. I think of the brain as running the body and your Higher Power or Universal Mind as running the whole show. Scientists have differing opinions on whether the mind is inside the body or outside. I personally think it's everywhere … but that doesn't matter.

There's no doubt that artistic creators like you and me tap into the Universal Mind or Universal Intelligence in order to access innovative, unique, and surprising ideas. In the current technology us creativity junkies also have Artificial Intelligence to tap into. A.I. is pretty amazing, but is not the deep well you get from the Universal Mind/Intelligence.

Dr. Einstein was known to discover secrets of the Universe after a nap. The superpowers of the mind are not out there, but within your mind ... where your Higher Power also resides.

*** **Technology**—As an aside, intelligent technology is a valuable partner that could be explored. While technology is admirable it doesn't exist without humans to program their intelligence into it or take it's creative data and adapt it to a desired outcome. Robots can interchange programmed words, ideas, and processes to appear intelligent and original but it's not original thought ... it's an artificial copy. A.I. can't think, or access original, spiritual, or creative intelligence for new and unique solutions. That's your part and we are partners.

Keep in mind that robots or artificial intelligence have no feelings or emotions. It's usually your emotions that drive your actions. Robots don't care about you or anything beyond what they've been programmed to do ... put together language systems as a tool for your benefit. In my experience, the artificial intelligence I've used is excellent and is a powerful tool when used for creativity.*

Create the Space for a Partnership

There are two steps to solidifying a Spiritual Partnership. The first simple step of *asking* can be life changing. You absolutely must "ask" for guidance, for your inner Teacher to be on your team, or for help in your partnership. Don't beg or plead ... just ask in a sincere way because with the asking, your life will most likely change. Remember the quote, *"With God all things are possible."*

*** **Fuel**—I was new to ACIM when I read an early passage suggesting I invite Guidance into my life. I instantly got up from my chair, walked to my bedroom, got on my knees, and asked through prayer for Guidance. It was as simple as that! Did I receive guidance? Yes, and more! These simple actions fueled my inner Spiritual and outer physical life. My dreams became more vivid and instructive and my inner Voice directed me in ways to set me up for a different lifestyle. I was ready! Are you ready for that level of change? If you are committed to learning your life purpose and enhancing your relationship with the Divine, then know your life will change. If you prefer to coast along, then continue to coast, but you'll miss the adventure!

The second step is to start your Spiritual practice if you haven't already done so. You asked for guidance in the first step. This second step will put you in the position to listen ... or hear from the Divine during your meditations or whenever it's needed. These two steps together are the actions that speed up or fuel your Spiritual Awakening and lead into the right and perfect awareness of your Ideal Life Path!*

*** **The Beginning**—My spiritual practice began when I was in my mid twenties. You'll read my personal story of how it helped me overcome my reliance on drugs ... thereby saving my life. You'll gain subtle guidance from your inner Guide when your mind is quiet, open, and not distracted with noise. It could be during your naps, quiet nature walks, during long boring drives, mental quiet times, while you're doing something routine like taking a shower or bath, or meditating. Be open to surprising spontaneous responses.

The million-dollar question is whether you are hearing sacred Guidance or ego-dum guidance? Ego guidance is usually 'me-oriented' and fearful. If you're uncertain, always give extra thought to what you heard. Then determine if your guidance sounds aligned with previous interactions with your Higher Power.*

Co-Creation and Creativity

Tap into the One Universal Mind for all your creative needs just by focusing on your project and giving it some of your mental time and space. Welcome creativity and mind expansion by extending an invitation and opening the door.

Giving birth to your Ideal Life Path or creative endeavors is a natural process guided by destiny. You're not supposed to struggle. Remember that your creative ideas are coming through you and it's your part in the co-creation process to give birth to those sacred ideas.

Also keep in mind that some creative paths may not be suitable for you. As much as you enjoy watercolor painting, songwriting, or writing non-fiction it might not be a match for you. Pay particular attention to what does bring you joy and stick with that. Success is more likely.

As a reminder, co-create your Ideal Life Path in alignment with your Higher Power's will. ACIM ascertains that both wills are the same and aligning yourself with that idea will save you some heartache. Your open mind and inner guidance come together to co-create a heart-centered experience to be made manifest in the world.

If your personal Dream doesn't manifest, a different one will. Your next step will be to learn what it is and follow that path instead. Be open minded and look to a brighter future, one that is meant for you.

*** **Next!**—I once had a Dream to become a flight attendant for an airline company. I felt ecstatic when the opportunity arrived to interview for the position. I was flown to Chicago but it was one of those days that nothing went my way. I later discovered I hadn't even put my underwear on right that morning. I wasn't surprised when I didn't get the job. It was not my Higher Power's will for me. Was I disappointed? Yes, but I said to myself, "next!"*

*** **Disappointment**—I once applied for a position at U.C. Berkeley as an administrative assistant. I had the necessary experience, the school was close to home, and there was an opportunity to finish my degree on campus over time. I felt excitement when I discovered I registered #2 out of 200 applicants. Grogginess overcame me by not sleeping the night before. I didn't ace the interview. I had to let it go.*

Spirit Supports You in All Ways

As I have said before, you are not alone in your guided endeavors. I believe that the Universe gives you a chance to reach your Dreams, but they don't always manifest or they may be realized at a future time. Beyond that, you have all the support of Heaven within you, and for that, you offer your faith, trust, and willingness to take action. Remember, Dreams don't manifest in a day ... usually!

The Miracle-Minded tune in to what's coming to you and through you, just like I did when I heard the word *"typography."* I'll repeat an important clue: notice if your thoughts and perceptions are repetitive in a non-intrusive and subtle way. *Notice specific words or ideas and start to question their meaning or place in your life.* This is normally how your inner Teacher communicates with you when you're guided to do something specific. Be mindful of that. Spirit totally supports you but not in a way that could frighten you. It's usually subtle.

Guiding thoughts come to you in a way to get your attention and not bombard you. This is not your ego we're talking about here. It's Higher Power Wisdom, and is generally subtle although not always so. There are times when your inner Teacher will move you along quicker than what you might expect and it can be uncomfortable. My personal story below shares my experience with a quick shift from upside down thinking to Miracle-Mindedness.

*** **Dark Night of Soul**—I've talked to people who've reported, and I've experienced it for myself, a 'dark night of the soul' experience. It's sometimes labeled as a 'Spiritual emergency or Spiritual emergence.' This sometimes happens during a transformational life experience. I believe it's meant to shake you up and turn you around ... a breakdown in values, thereby getting you in alignment with your Higher Power's will.

If you have this experience and find it disturbing, you might consider professional help. Even though I found 'the dark night' to be a challenging experience, I eventually considered it to be a gift. My breakdown in values promptly kicked me out of my assumptions and delusions to place me on my rightful path. Co-creating means looking for the good or the gifts in even the darkest situation.*

SUCCESS SKILLS

Developing your Spiritual awareness is an ongoing skill that offers a profound (ROI) Return On Investment that pays off over your lifetime. Daily listening and meditation is key. You'll learn how your Higher Power is working with you in your life. As a co-creator, you'll develop a level of wisdom and access to truth you weren't aware of before. It's like turning on a light in a dark room. All of a sudden you can see more clearly and understand situations that may have previously seemed confusing.

A Tool for Your Personal Growth

How does it help your confidence to know that your Dream (s) are a gift from the Universe for your happiness? How does it make you feel to know you are getting assistance from your Higher Power or your Divine Helpers?

Develop Your Inner Resources

The Miracle-Minded know that developing your inner Resources is critical to achieving your Higher Power's will. This partnership allows you to co-create through your inner Teacher ... who mediates between you and your Higher Power. Many individuals in the Miracle-Minded community call their inner Teacher the Holy Spirit. Use whatever name you're comfortable with but that's what the Miracle-Minded learn through ACIM.

The ultimate goal of your inner Resource is to align your thoughts, perceptions, and goals to be on the same wavelength. Working together is the best way. You may be guided to take classes, follow a particular teacher, or read Spiritual books. I believe I was guided to live in San Francisco to study under a particular teacher and be a part of his Spiritual Community. I could not have learned ACIM or had the experiences I needed to have in any other place.

Resources may guide you to learn self-help/personal growth techniques. Don't hold back if you've never done any self-help work in your past. It's revealing! All inner work calls for courage, open mindedness, and the willingness to go beyond perceived limitations. Everything you learn here can be used throughout the rest of your life journey. Achievement in personal growth is found by moving through the pain and disappointment of a career or relationship failure to the other side where you learned what it takes to make a better decision.

If you've ever read any fiction, you know his/her story begins when you learn your hero has a big problem or conflict. Throughout his or her journey they have experiences that both hurt and help them. It's only through those changes that their story ending becomes a happier one. Allow yourself to experience the Heroes Journey so you can achieve happiness now.

My first story of how my inner Teacher guided my career was an example of how that works. I heard and followed an inner Voice. That experience expanded my horizons and allowed me to move past fears that held me captive.

Your inner Teacher is designed to direct you to all that your Higher Power has in store for you. It might be a college degree, a specific vacation or pilgrimage, or a problem solved.

Yes, ACIM says there's a Storehouse waiting for you. This entire chapter spells out the way, through your Divine inner Resources into that Storehouse. Ask about it in your meditation time. You may have friends and family who do their best to help you overcome your hurdles, but your loving support system goes beyond the human form. As one who is Miracle-Minded, you'll learn that Spiritual awareness is pretty much of a super power. Shifts happen and synchronicities occur as you use your super power to co-create your Ideal Life Path.

Shifting into a positive mindset, regardless of what you're going through, puts you into alignment and unity to co-create with your Higher Power.

Get Grounded in Spirit

"The mind has a natural urge to find life meaningful." Deepak Chopra, author

Are you aware that some of your Dreams and fantasies are ego-related ... such as winning the lottery or Publishers Clearinghouse? You don't really have a strong passion for Dreams like real estate mogul, hedge fund manager, or high-end restaurateur ... just to be wealthy. You don't have any intention of working that hard or bringing those fantasies to life. It's more like a "nice to have." Those fantasies are a total waste of time ... mentally and emotionally.

Ground yourself in your intuition, Spiritual practice, and personal growth work. These are steps that count and can get you to your Ideal Life Path, better relationships, and a happier future. I promise to share these clues:

1. You'll learn how to pinpoint the difference between your Dream and a Big Dream.

2. You'll also learn a magic word!

You don't necessarily have to leave your current job/career in order to explore promises of more happiness or a higher level of creativity and satisfaction! You can learn from key words/search engines on the internet, interview someone who is experienced, or read the critical facts in a book before you move forward on an illusive idea.

The better alternative is to get grounded in the direction your inner Teacher is leading you, which may or may not include a departure from your current career. Put your feet on the ground, your sights on your Higher Power, and a future filled with light and happiness!!

You can have many creative Dreams throughout your life and they have different levels of significance. Exploring a path that calls to you can lead to interesting adventures and happy outcomes. The trick is in noticing when you are called and believing that you have been called. And of course the most important step is deciding to take action.

*** **Co-Creation**—Synchronicity and one magic word changed my life. One holiday season I temporarily worked at a large department store in San Francisco. When business was slow the independent contractors in my department would chat. I mentioned to a co-worker, *"I wanted a job that was more meaningful than handing out samples and selling a product that many West Coast people didn't appreciate ... fragrances."*

As my luck would have it, he immediately introduced me to his friend who was looking for an administrative assistant. I had administrative experience, applied for the position, and was hired. Meaningful was the magic word. In hindsight I realized my Higher Power and I co-created an opportunity for me to shift into a solid and gratifying position. I would be of support to help people quit using tobacco products, save their health, and maybe their lives.*

BIG Dreams, Bigger Changes!

Your Dreams can change with the wind and some are more grounded. Remember your grounded Dreams are the ones where you have the passion, knowledge, and intention. You can call those three characteristics potential. It's your commitment that can change your life and the world in powerful ways. I wanted to help people become non-smokers!

What Do You Want?

And then there is what I call the Big Dream: the one that changes not only your life, but the lives of others too. There were many people throughout history who had a Big Dream and made BIG changes! I immediately think of Albert Einstein, Mahatma Gandhi, and Franklin D. Roosevelt, along with Jesus, Buddha, and many others. More currently, those who stand out are Steve Jobs, Bill Gates, Martin Luther King Jr. and even Elvis Presley, and the pop musical group, the Beatles. The list is long and a Big Dream is possible in most any career.

My mission is to encourage everyone who is Miracle-Minded to take action when they're called! Discover or rediscover your important Dream ... the one that makes your heart sing.

* **Wave Your Wand!** I discovered the magic word is *"meaningful!"* Using that word in a sincere way is like waving a magic wand. *"I want to do something meaningful"* or *"Meaningful work is important to me!"* *"I want a meaningful relationship!"* The Universe hears your words, feels your heart ... and responds.*

Is your Big Dream meaningful ... having the potential to help many people? If you experienced a Big Dream and it's "a Divinely Inspired Whopper," then you might want to spend more time listening to your wise inner Voice. The world needs you!

SUCCESS SKILLS

Becoming mentally and Spiritually grounded are two skills you'll want to include in your interpretation of a realistic Dream or Ideal Life Path.

Tools for Your Personal Growth

1. What Dreams feel grounded to you? What makes them so? Write that into your journal.

2. Use this brief visualization to meet your inner Guide/Teacher:

Before you go to sleep tonight, as you are lying on your bed, take a few deep breaths to feel centered within your body. As you relax your body, create your intention to connect with your Inner Guide or the Teacher within. Ask if your inner Guide will be revealed to you? Ask for your Guide to tell you his/her name and to reveal him/her self. Ask if the Guide has been with you since birth or more recently. Ask if the Guide is a benevolent entity? Ask if the Guide can help you with your Ideal Life Path or Purpose?

Wait for a reply and if you aren't able to receive anything now, be patient as the answer can come at any time. You may also allow yourself to fall asleep and awake with your answers.

A Tool for Your Personal Growth - Your Storehouse

In a previous chapter we talked about what you're meant to be, do, and learn. Imagine a Storehouse of experiences that are meant for you. What Divine gifts would you receive from your own personal Storehouse?

Your Next Steps

This was a solid chapter moving you forward to co-create your Ideal Life Path with your Higher Power. These chapters are preparing you for what's to come. They'll help you lay a foundation upon which to build the inner Spiritual strength you'll have for a lifetime. Just know that what you're asked to do will help you become stronger in your Spiritual life and your relationship with your Higher Power.

CHAPTER THIRTEEN

THE PROCESS OF DISCOVERY

"Learn to honor your deep and complex story."
Lisa Congdon, artist, author of *"You Will Leave a Trail of Stars."*

This is the point where you dig deeper into your own life and honor where you've been and where you're likely to go. This is your Process of Discovery, where you'll mine your past, present, and future for the seeds of destiny or greatness that you may have overlooked. As your Spiritual Midwife, I'll help you water those seeds so you can identify them now as what they truly are ... highly valuable golden nuggets leading to your Ideal Life Path!

In the beginning chapters you looked inside yourself. You hopefully healed any misperceptions that disempowered your life and kept you in the struggle and suffering mode. You found pure gold in the tools that transformed you. In earlier chapters you also learned about the tremendous powers of your mind and how to access them as tools for sowing what you need. You then connected with your Higher Power through meditation, inner listening, aligning, and co-creating with your Higher Power. Your connection with your Higher Power is more valuable than pure gold.

You learned to pay attention to your dreams to receive greater insight on your next steps. The last chapter connected you with your inner Resources and made it clear that you are not alone. You have a valuable support system ... the golden light within that Divinely supports you.

WHY IS THIS IMPORTANT?

You know by now that if you want to be led to your Ideal Life Path, you have to go to a higher authority first ... your Higher Power. And then check in again before making a decision. The way I look at it, if doors open for you, it's most likely a good decision ... at least for now.

When you think about it, new career adventures or the next chapter of your life are both discoveries and mysteries to be revealed, unfolded, or solved. There's a natural process of discovery that happens whether you're exploring the potential of a life partner, a new baby, a different home, a new Spiritual path or your long-held Dreams. You'll go forth, step-by-step to discover the next piece of the puzzle and see how it fits into the overall picture of your life.

I'll take you deeper into your past, present, and even your future. You'll mine your life experiences (like I've done), look deeply at your intentions, and answer questions to help you define and measure your enthusiasm/emotions.

Honor Your Life Experiences

In previous chapters I gave you honest stories of how my Higher Power worked in my life. My stories showed how the Divine led me to my own best interests. This chapter focuses on you, your discoveries, and what you may bring to the party. Well, some of us are working on building "Heaven on Earth." Please join us for the party!

In this chapter you're going to do a life review and explore your past, present, and future dreams and fantasies. By mining these important areas of your life you may find clues and discoveries to where your Higher Power is leading you. Remember the sacred seed I talked about in the beginning? There have been clues all along, especially when you explored the content of your dreams and meditations. There may be some clues you missed and we'll look for them.

Focusing on a happy future and what you think you want or need is an important and insightful activity that needs to happen now. Look to your happier life and discover your rightful place in the world. *"Where do I start?"* is a great question.

You already started when you began reading the introduction. You started a process of looking at your life possibly in a way you never have before. I suspect that at some point you Course-Corrected to the best of your ability. You've learned how to go within and listen through your meditation practice. You've discovered ways to connect, align, and co-create with your Creator. You know how to interpret when your dreams are Spiritual and significant, and you know the power of your subconscious and super-conscious mind.

You've come a long way from the beginning. By using the Tools for Personal Growth, you've taken solid steps to build a strong foundation with your Higher Power. That foundation and connection can help you uncover that sacred seed within you and grow it into it's full flowering.

This chapter is designed to help you answer the next question, *"What is my Ideal Life Path?"* Through self-inquiry, you'll be led to many possibilities and viable options. I've included story examples to assist you. I've often reminded you that you are a co-creator with your Higher Power, but that doesn't mean you can't use technology or career services to stimulate ideas for your Ideal Life Path. Indeed, you should explore all ideas or options no matter what they are or where you received them. Turn them over to your Higher Power for approval.

*** **Research**—In the beginning of my midlife career search, I spent a fair amount of time researching and exploring various careers for myself. It allowed me to scratch off the ideas I knew weren't a match. I didn't want any regrets and if one is curious, nothing should be off-limits. There was no internet then, so I used the resources available to me. Also keep in mind that I was not particularly Miracle-Minded at that time. I casually read metaphysical and self-help books and practiced meditation, but was not formally following any Spiritual or religious path. This means that I looked to Guidance for direction.*

No doubt, there are many ways to get direction from the outside world. You can go to the internet job boards to search: LinkedIn, Indeed, Craig's List, ZipRecruiter, Job.com, Glassdoor, CareerBuilder etc. to see what jobs/careers exist in the labor market. Colleges, Universities, temps jobs, recruiters, and other career search sites might be able to lead you toward a hopeful career, but not necessarily your Ideal Life Path. They don't know your place in your Higher Power's plan, so the result may be more years of wasted time, money, and effort to find yourself in another dead end job.

I know the standard route works for some people but not for those with a higher calling. And on the other hand, there are no accidents. To be open-minded, a job or position you come across in your search could be a key to unlock the door of a promising career choice and your Ideal Life Path. Follow all leads while paying attention to your level of enthusiasm: a strong passion/energy.

Stretch Your Imagination

What is the Imagination? It's the field of possibility beyond this physical world where you can tap into the well of creativity and the almighty will of the Divine super-conscious mind. You can discover your imagination. It's the power and creative energy over all that exists that creates like itself: love, light, and wisdom.

To stretch your imagination is to go within, be who you are so you can experience your own creative self-expression through words and images.

Getting to the future you desire may include thinking outside the box! One of the Ideal Life Path Seekers' biggest frustrations is becoming an open and active receiver of the Universal expansive intuition and imagination. You keep trying and nothing happens. That's why I've spent so much time encouraging you to build a Spiritual foundation and grow Spiritually, so you can tap into your *Field of Dreams:*

1. Become more mindful or Miracle-Minded. Continue your inner listening practice or go deeper with your current Spiritual practice. Try to get to the theta level of mind for hearing your inner Voice.

2. Listen for guidance from your wise inner Voice. Always be patient and mindful during your meditations, early morning sleep state, and dreams ... the three Gateways. Wait for *your awareness of an inner shift, from conscious mind to super-conscious mind.*

3. Connect with your Higher Power through prayer.

4. Keep remembering who you are, a Spiritual being having a human experience.

Discipline is the Name of the Game!

Be focused and disciplined. Clear your mind of useless ranting and constant spinning about your past. It takes up too much of your 1) precious time and 2) space in your thinking mind that could be used for bigger and better outcomes.

You've prepared yourself Spiritually for your Ideal Life Path. All throughout this program you've answered important questions about yourself within the Tools for Personal Growth. You're slowly awakening to who you really are and the power, love, and strength that lies within your mind, heart, and core. Be disciplined, open-minded, and persistent so it's easier to access the wisdom and creativity in your imagination.

Access Your Inner Genius

By aligning, connecting, and co-creating with your Higher Power you discover and earn the gift of inner genius. I like to translate the word "genius" into the "genie in us." Of course there's no real genie, but the actualization of the *Spirit of genius* may sometimes feel like there is. That's when Spirit's gifts come to you from out of the blue. Or creative ideas start flowing. Accessing your creative genius or active imagination is a major factor if you want to be known as a creative to get ahead in life or in your field of opportunity.

Upgrading your creative genius skills may help you find creative solutions to any hurdles in your way. Hurdles could be: relationship issues, finding the best location for your new business, connecting with someone who has a large social media following or popular podcast. You might discover a publisher for your new book, online business, or song. It's your intuition and imagining faculties, like an antenna and a funnel, that must receive and download energetic vibrations from your super-conscious mind. Immersion, constant practice, and repetition are like a magnet for creative innovation from the ethers.

There are no limits to what you can accomplish if you let go of control and go inward to make the space for new thoughts and perceptions and for synchronicities to occur. Otherwise it's the same old sad story.

You'll read in the next chapter that this book and program is the result of synchronicity, an orderly opening of doors dependent on a commitment to one's pursuit of meaning. Synchronicities are usually a series of messages from the Universe letting you know that you are on the right path. Experiences, events, and extraordinary people line up along your path to show you the way. Doors open to save you time.

"Synchronicity is an ever present reality for those who have eyes to see."
Carl Jung

Imagine Your Mind on Daydreams and Fantasies!

Do you sometimes sit back, relax, and ask, *"What if?"* You might have a daydream or fantasy that takes you somewhere else, perhaps outside of yourself. What if you decided to go to Paris on your next vacation instead of your usual camping trip? What if you took that class you've been fascinated with? What if you treated your significant other to flowers, dinner, a spa treatment, or a concert instead of watching a movie at home?

You are dreaming up your life every single day with each thought and decision you make. You might as well make it pleasant for yourself and others. You may start your day by looking at your phone and its calendar or your to do list. Those actions start your daily journey into the world you made up for yourself. Your choices and decisions throughout the day, sometimes moment by moment, can take you in any number of directions. Of course there are also random situations that pop up: an unexpected invitation to lunch, car trouble, or a friend in need. That's okay and in Divine order.

Start your day differently for it to unfold in a more surprising manner.

These are practices for stretching your imagination as well as stretching your daily joy. It's only a matter of time before your subconscious and super-conscious mind support you in your endeavors.

1. Start with a prayer or a blessing.

2. Repeatedly ask your Higher Power for an experience you want.

3. Practice a brief meditation or quiet listening and deep breathing.

4. Do a visual rehearsal of the kind of day you want to experience, (beautiful, peaceful, or purposeful) or how you'll shine your light with everyone you meet: the bus driver, barista, or waitress?

5. Slow down and start listening and looking within for signs of direction: an image, a hunch, intuition, or an unexpected gift.

6. Read an inspirational passage, email, poem, or listen to inspiring music. Randomly turn to a page in your favorite inspirational book to see if there's a special message for you.

Neuroscientists agree that you can change your brain by learning something new and/or taking new actions. You are inviting neurons to wire/fire together and that in itself helps you build a better brain and become smarter at the same time.

Can You Imagine Happiness Now?

There may be times in your life when the intent of your daydreams shift from the mundane to the miraculous. You can measure your level of happiness about something you desire: a home, romantic partner, or a travel opportunity.

Determine those levels on a scale of one to ten with one being a low level of joy and ten being the highest level of happiness. Be open minded about your potential for change and the possibility of becoming more in alignment with a top life-changing desire, a #10.

Daydreaming, fantasizing, or making up a life that inspires you is an important exercise in pinpointing options and potential for a happy life. It's about co-creating with your Higher Power and living out a long held Dream that brings you joy. Remember that you spread your light lavishly when you take that joy into the world with you.

Dream yourself into a career that you may seriously be interested in pursuing. You may Dream of becoming a chef who opens his or her new restaurant, a policeman/woman who gets the beat they want, or a dancer who intends to travel to New York City for an exciting Broadway career.

Use your imagination and actually see yourself rehearsing a particular role. Do the work and notice how you feel about it, how you struggle or succeed. Because you are consciously making this up, it doesn't mean it isn't valid or valuable. It's an exercise in creative self-expression.

You may spontaneously talk with someone, a friend or stranger, who shares how interesting, rewarding, or challenging their career is. You could learn about a certain career in high school or college and do research on pay, hours, creativity, benefits, and overall satisfaction. Because one person you interview loves their field doesn't mean you will too. There are many variables to look at along with education, knowledge, passion, gifts, temperament etc.

You may find that some of your Dreams and fantasies are ego-related. You don't have a strong passion for them or any intention of bringing them to life. It's more like a "nice to have."

Most importantly, know that anything is possible and your fantasy may be in alignment with your Higher Power's will for you. Many people receive immense gratification from having their own bakery, woodworking shop or yoga studio. Whatever you and your Higher Power decide on, it's always about your happiness and His.

SUCCESS SKILLS

The skill of being grounded is one you'll want to include in your interpretation of a realistic Ideal Life Path.

Tools for Your Personal Growth

Tool #1: Look back on your day to see how many times you changed your mind and soon changed your direction.

Tool #2: On a scale of one to ten, how would you measure your current happiness: career, home life, religion, or spirituality? What number is your relationship with your significant other, your children, family, co-workers, health, and community?

Tool #3: Pay attention to conversations you have with different people. There may be synchronicities. I noticed that once I started to write this Learn Your Life Purpose book, people began sharing their life journeys with me. Their stories gave me inspiration for this book.

Tool #4: What career or life do you find yourself fantasizing about? Do you have a budding talent for that career? Dream BIG!

Tool #5: Expand your mind by reading books on creativity. Stretching your mind/imagination is the same idea as stretching your body. Play around with the idea of Yoga for Your Mind! Move your mind/thoughts around by varying your thoughts ... think differently! How can you do this or that differently, better, or longer? What problems can you solve?

Creativity is perfect for writers, artists, or scientists etc. Can you go in another direction? Can you stretch a little further this time? Have you discovered something fascinating or inspiring while traveling in foreign countries? Stretch the context of your ideas. Plant some seeds. It may not be easy in the beginning, but give your subconscious mind time to pull unique ideas together for you. Write here about any advances you've discovered.

Visionary Experiences

Visions are snapshots of the unknown or your future! Visions can be extraordinary experiences and significant to the imaginary process. I don't think they happen everyday, at least not to me. If your super-conscious mind gives you one, it can be an important insight into your future.

*** **Creative Visions**—Shortly after moving to San Francisco in the1990's I had a rare experience of an outward vision. I think of this oddity as a minor supernatural experience. It wasn't earth shattering, but certainly surprising.

I was working on a creative project and experienced some difficulty with the design. All of a sudden a perfect vision of the completed object, an ornate Native American candle, appeared to me as I sat there thinking about it. The surprise was that the vision didn't happen in my inner mind as it usually does when I dream or meditate. I saw the finished product outside of me, in front of my open eyes. It reminded me of a scene in a science fiction movie. This experience happened only once, and actually quite astounded me!

I sense that these random supernatural experiences are hints regarding our human potential and what can happen when we somehow slip into the realm of our super-conscious mind.*

*** **Bugsy**—Sometimes a vision may foretell the future. In the 1991 movie, "Bugsy," Warren Beatty played the role of the gangster, Benjamin/Bugsy Siegel. The story revealed what appeared to be a supernatural experience. The movie, Bugsy, told the story of the mob boss's foray into building a gambling casino in the Nevada desert. According to the movie, he drove through the desert and eventually stopped the car to get out and empty his bladder. When he looked up, he had a vision of the future Las Vegas. He came back to his car excited about what he saw. This story may be true or a Hollywood addition. *

To his credit, Bugsy later built the Flamingo hotel and casino in the dessert area of Las Vegas. It was not an immediate success and Bugsy lost his life due to his inability to pay his debts. We all know what that vision led to and many people enjoy what Las Vegas has become. It's not just a gambling paradise, but another entertainment capital of the world visited by millions of people throughout the world.

Your North Star: A Supernatural Vision

You may or may not have a Supernatural Vision. If you do, it may come in the form of a nighttime dream or a daydream. You may have a vision of the future for yourself, for an organization or business, or all three. It's basically a snapshot about where you and/or the business aspires to go or what it aspires to achieve.

Similar to other important insights, a vision serves as a North Star and pathway to some great achievement. It's a picture of what could be ... possibilities! Typically, real visions are not fantasies but are a Spiritual experience. You might have a vision of yourself in the future as a popular politician, a sought after character actor, or successful jazz musician. Some people focus on their passion or what Joseph Campbell, the famous Mythologist, called *"your bliss!"* Your passion or bliss will lead you toward a certain outcome and it may or may not be your purpose. It may be a detour. You'll need to explore that possibility.

SUCCESS SKILLS

Necessary skills for your process of discovery is being open-minded and allowing your imagination to soar! Some choices and decisions in life require courage and faith. Courage can be a difficult skill to achieve, but with faith, it lessens the fear involved. Remember ... take one step at a time!

Tools for Your Personal Growth

Tool #1: During your meditation practice, when you are relaxed and comfortable, visualize yourself achieving a long held Dream. Does it feel right?

Tool #2: Have you experienced any kind of vision? If so, write it down in as much detail as you can remember. Does it excite you? What steps could you take to manifest this vision? What did you learn?

Tool #3: Have you ever felt Spiritually called to do, be, or learn about something you previously desired? If so, what small steps would you take if you had more courage and even more faith?

* I suggest writing as much as you can on one sheet of paper so you can view the big picture, similar to a mind map.

Discover Your Ideal Life Path

These are the three steps you'll take to discover Your Ideal Life Path!
Search Your Soul:

    Step One: Mine Your Past for Clues

    Step Two: Mine Your Present for Clues

    Step Three: Mine Your Future for Clues

Your Soul Speaks of Your Destiny—Your Higher Ideal

If there were no Divine plan, then you are here at random and the chances of you even having a destiny or a calling would be questionable. In fact, the whole idea would be totally up to you to implement with no inside assistance or very sketchy outside help.

The good news is you've learned through the Miracle-Minded that *"chance plays no part in God's plan"* (ACIM: M-9.3). So a pre-determined Divine plan must, at some point, reveal your part/role to you. It's your soul's purpose to set you up, prepare you, and lead you to discover what was once a Sacred Seed. That sacred seed has now become your Dreams, Calling, or Life Purpose. Are you ready to search your soul and then present your findings to the world? Fear not! You are not alone!

*** MIDWIFE CHAPTERS

Midwife Chapter #One: I knew a forty-ish year old woman who was pretty much clueless about ever having an Ideal Life Path. She achieved her initial Dream of owning her own business, and she was looking for a new happy occupation/Dream for the next chapter of her life ... one with less stress and responsibility. She didn't even think about a Big Dream, Vision, Mission, or Life Purpose. None of those concepts were in her vocabulary or on her mind when she decided to move on from a challenging but long and fulfilling career. She just wanted to do something *more with her life:* make a good living to support herself, be productive, and find happiness in her life experiences and adventures. That woman was me!

Midwife Chapter #Two: One day in early 1990, I sat down and intuitively created a plan that would help me find *Happiness Now!* That plan is what you're about to learn. I first remembered my childhood when I was around 10 years old. There were several life paths I had been enthusiastic about. Some were too unrealistic for me, like becoming the cowgirl I saw on television Westerns. I became infatuated with that idea until the first and second time I actually rode a horse. Whoa, the scary and bumpy ride halted that Dream!

I also briefly dreamed of becoming a minister, until I discovered women could be nuns but not ministers. Nuns were restricted: no marriage or children. That was a non-starter for me and I didn't know enough to know there were other options and other churches. Ministry became a Dream I finally achieved.

I remembered that over my young adult years I dabbled in and found joy in three different areas: various artistic endeavors, baking and party planning, and creative writing. I was way too busy with my small business to pursue these beloved hobbies in any depth. That was about to change.

I figured a career I enjoyed and also supported me financially would automatically be my future. Imagine my surprise when my future found me!

Midwife Chapter #Three: Most everything I'll share with you from this point forward was a total surprise to me, even that I wanted to make a difference in the world! Where did that come from? I'll share a glimpse of the surprising and mysterious Chapter #Three, along with more coaching on learning your Ideal Life Path!

Points to Focus on and Remember!

You're now going to take the exact same three magical steps I took to not only search your soul but to follow your heart, as well as your inner Guidance.

    1. Search Your Soul - your holistic awareness

    2. Look into Your Heart - your deeper truth

    3. Follow Your Guidance - the wisdom of the Divine

To define your long held Dreams or future, you'll explore three important areas of your life: your past, your present, and yes, even your future.

Point #1: Mine Your Past for Clues

SEARCH YOUR SOUL

1. Mine Your Past! Search your soul for options that interested or excited you over the years, starting with your childhood and then your teen years. The seeds of what you loved then may still be growing inside you. They may be ready to take form!

Take the time to answer these questions if you really want to learn your Ideal Life Path! To read on and not do the work will make this whole process a failure. Please write your answers into this book or your journal and they'll stimulate your subconscious mind, intuition, and imagination.

1. What were you curious about in your childhood or teen years?

2. What talents or interests came naturally: cooking, art, building things, taking care of animals, repairing cars, making your own clothes, computers, selling things, etc?

3. What were the hobbies or activities you enjoyed the most: baseball, ballet, or sewing, gardening, acting in school plays, etc.?

4. What were you introduced to that has a possibility for a career: football, golf, hockey, dance, writing, science, video games, dress making for dolls or for yourself?

5. What did you enjoy doing or learning at these ages?

Up to age 10

Ages 11 – 13

Ages 14 – 18

2. Think it through and visualize yourself in various positions. How does it look and feel? What are your thoughts? Are you comfortable or do you feel like a fish out of water? Find no more than 4-5 career choices that you were attracted to in your childhood or teenage/young adult years. Remember, with Miracle-Minded thinking, any hobby can be transformed into a career path.

List those here:

1.

2.

3.

4.

5.

LEARN YOUR LIFE PURPOSE

3. Make a list of all the pros and cons that come to mind for each career option. Do some research to discover what other people say are pros and cons. Look them over and eliminate any career paths you can't live with.

PRO's   CON's
1.
2.
3.
4.
5.

Tools for Your Personal Growth

Tool #1: Spend some time remembering your past: youth or young adult fantasies. What inspires you to explore a certain field further?

Tool #2: Visualize Your Childhood Fantasies

Read through the following visualization first. Read it a second time and give yourself the experience.

* Find a quiet place to sit and relax. Sit in a chair with both feet on the floor and your hands in your lap, palms facing upward. Take several deep breaths with your eyes closed.

Allow your body to relax. Start with your feet and name each section of your body, commanding your body parts in each area to let go and relax. Finish up with the top of your head.

Imagine yourself going within and visualizing a time in your young life when you were excited to become a part of something larger than yourself. You dreamed about achieving goals that felt would bring you joy. Go back to those very moments and see your youthful self in your minds' eye. See yourself as you felt excitement, joy, and magnetism. You said to yourself, *"I want to do or be that when I grow up!"* Remember that very moment, and open your mind and heart to feeling that same excitement.

Continue to feel the joy inside your body. Allow your joy to permeate every part of you, from your toes to the top of your head. Bask in the joy! When you're ready, open your eyes and come back into the room.

Bring the remembrance of this experience back with you. Write it down and investigate how this visualization could manifest in your current life.

4. Narrow your list down to three possibilities.

Investigate the potential for joy and other requirements in each option from your youth or teen years. List your three priorities and think about what they offer you in the way of job satisfaction and work/life balance.

Which one has the best chance of being chosen and why?
1.
2.
3.

Point #2: Mine Your Present for Clues

You may already be doing something that is a possibility for your Big Dream or Ideal Life Path. You might be taking a course, working on a side hustle or gig, or helping someone else with a project that you could take on for yourself at some point. What are you doing at this moment that brings you joy? What are you thinking about doing that excites you?

You may be retired and remember that there was always something else you wanted to do with your life, but something else was always a priority. Maybe you wanted to start a business, but needed to take care of your family first, or you lacked the education you needed, or the money, or the motivation? You now have the time and a bit of savings to invest in a long-held Dream. Begin with those fantasies in mind, and weigh them for their potential

*** **A Road Sign**—Once I sold my business I immediately gravitated toward writing my first non-fiction book. It included information I wish I had known when I started that business. Other business owners would find it helpful. That was my first big clue and road sign that writing was my right path. As a side note … it's still my most popular selling non-fiction book.*

Question Your Desires & Motivations

1. Take into account the typical work location to learn if it's a match for you.
You may not want to drive a great distance to work in a city location or a country location. Study environmental pros and cons or any dangers your choices may have. Would you have to stand all day, get up earlier than what you're comfortable with, or earn less money? Allow some practicality into your decisions, but be open to a change of mind or your passion winning out.

2. Keep in mind that technology continues to change and that fact may change things up for you. Artificial intelligence is currently sweeping the world and many people want to learn the ways of this new technology. Always investigate how careers and technology are changing before you make a decision.

3. What are any potential consequences or surprises from your decisions?

4. Ask yourself some important questions about your options:

    1. Did you feel a sacred seed of destiny growing within you? Is it calling you at this time in your life, occupying your thoughts, or feeling like it's something that needs to be explored?

    2. Does it feel right to you now? What are your emotions telling you?

    3. How about if you served in the military, attended college or trade school? What stood out to you?

SUCCESS SKILLS

Use your imagining skills to see yourself in various careers. Be open-minded to every possibility. I suggest continuing your inner listening skills through meditation. An open-minded attitude led me to my degree (many years later) in the graphic arts. The Miracle-Minded always include their Higher Power in the equation!

*** Surprises—I studied my list and chose three suitable options. I came to a surprising and important realization after exploring my options in detail. *"I wanted to do something meaningful to make a difference in the world!"* Due to my age and life experience, my values had changed. I chose the one with the possibility of making a difference in the world! That was an important revelation and a priority that had profound consequences!*

* Changes—For example, there was a time when people who chose winemaking as a career had to purchase farmland, live on a large plot of rural land, and hire many farm workers. Fortunately, systems and technologies change things over time. Currently, anyone interested in the wine industry can purchase grapes from a list of growers and establish their own winery wherever they desire. Education, funding, and ambition may be the entry points. Look into everything to see how technology has changed it.*

Tools for Your Personal Growth

Tool #1: How committed are you to discovering your Ideal Life Path? If you're at the point in your life where you're asking about or pursuing a Dream, it's most likely the "time" for you to discover it and cross that bridge into new territory. Are you fully committed or only partially committed?

Tool #2: Open your mind to new possibilities.

- Reflect on what you're doing now or in your free time that you enjoy.
- What current hobbies or side hustles bring you pleasure?
- What needs do you see or experience in the marketplace that you could explore, replace, innovate, or reinvent?
- What could you do better or less expensively than someone else?
- How can you expand on needs or monetize them using current technologies?
- What skills do you have that could be expanded upon? How can you use them in different ways?
- What are people in other states or countries doing with similar ideas?

Tool #3: What experiences, books, and classes or courses appeal to you? Have you looked at educational opportunities as an entrance into a new career? Many are free or low cost.

Tool #4: What are you fantasizing about? Make up what you think you'd like to do or be. If you could wave a magic wand and become anything, what would that be?

Tool #5: What options are available to you within your time frame?

Tool #6: How often are you asking for clarity? Have you turned over your decision to your Higher Power for confirmation?

Tool #7: What two or three serious options from your present life could become your Ideal Life Path?

1.
2.
3.

Point #3: Mine Your Future for Clues

Your past and present explorations should help you discover possibilities for a promising new life path. That's the practical part. Did you find at least one career path that meets your needs and desires and is in alignment with your Higher Power? If you did, great! Continue on your path.

But what if you didn't get a sense of your Ideal Life Path? Don't fret. Do you have Dreams that you've held for a long time? They may play a part in your destiny. Take those with you in your prayers and meditations and ask if you should take steps toward accomplishing one of them.

It's time to shift gears! This coaching program is about going beyond what you've learned from the world. It's about searching your soul to discover a path to happiness and meaning. That means going deeper into your inquiries. Spend a bit more time in reflection.

Be open to receive guidance from your Higher Power to chart your course like I did. You'll use the powerful process of guided imagery to see yourself in the future. You'll mine possibilities that you did not previously discover.

*** **A New Chapter**—After selling a business I owned for 15 years, I realized I accumulated valuable skills such as marketing, speaking confidently with others, business acumen, and a discipline that could be transferred to other careers.

Like you did in this chapter, I made a list of occupations I dreamed about throughout the years. After researching them and choosing three, I traveled to various locations, trade schools, and universities to discover what was doable for me financially and time wise.

Ultimately, I decided I wanted to make a difference in people's lives. That decision changed everything for me and I chose the path to accomplish that. What statement can satisfy your commitment? To become a writer and inspire my readers seemed to fit the bill over my other options. Over time, I was guided and able to achieve all three of my Ideal Life Plan options. *

Tools for Your Personal Growth

Tool #1: Reconnect with Your Inner Guide

This can be a powerful exercise for reconnecting with your Higher Power or inner Guide. Take at least ten minutes to do a body scan naming your body parts from your head to your toes.

Visualize yourself walking down a set of ten well-lighted stairs. At the same time feel yourself going deeper as you count down from ten to one. At the bottom of the stairs, see yourself walking in a beautiful garden, eventually resting on a park bench. You see an image walking toward you surrounded by a beautiful golden glow.

Ask this image it's name and why it's here? Be patient for your answer. Ask if you may be shown your future self? Listen for the reply.

You may also ask other questions on your mind, such as revealing your Ideal Life Path, if you are not aware of it yet. Say good-bye when you are finished and thank your inner Guide for helping you. Count back up from one to ten, feeling wide-awake and alert at the count of ten. Open your eyes and stretch your body, perhaps taking notes on your experience. You may also do this exercise right before bedtime with the intention to awaken with your answers.

Tool #2: What did you learn about your Inner Guide and Ideal Life Path?

Tool #3: Write a Resume to the Universal Mind

It's a typical practice to put together a resume for any career position you find appropriate for you. But what if the Universe was your potential employer and didn't ask for any requirements to start? You'd be trained over time or readily meet any requirements.

- How would you describe your goal, skills, and experience as it pertains to your Ideal Life Path?

- Is it possible that you haven't discovered your Ideal Life Path, but have all the talents, skills, and ambition for what your Higher Power has in store for you? State in your cover letter that you're open to your Higher Power's recommendations. Let it be free-form, relaxed, and from your heart.

- At the same time be quiet, go within to clarify to yourself and the Universe what it is you think you want and how it might look to you. Your energy and intention in this exercise can attract clues, ideas, and insight into your Ideal Life Path.

- Know that the law of attraction works, and whatever outcomes you achieve are inspired by your honesty, sincerity, and commitment to your Higher Power's plan for your life.

- Give yourself 10-15 minutes to gain some clarity on this project. Take an additional 20 minutes or however much time you need to write your resume to the Universal Mind. Print it out and review it from time to time, making changes as necessary.

Tool #4: Create a Miracle—a shift in perception from fear to love

During your meditation sessions, tell the Universe you are open to a life path that is in your own best interests. Use your imagining, open mindedness, and listening skills to experience the miracle meant for you. Use the former meditation once again to see an image of yourself in the future. That could be your clue about a direction to take.

Chart Your Course

Having found your Ideal Life Path by mining your past, present, and future, know that you'll be Spiritually guided to your next steps. Your guidance may or may not happen during the reading of this book or during the upcoming course: *"Learn Your Life Purpose."* The seed has been planted, you've done your homework, and in the right and perfect time you'll be led to your Ideal Life Path.

Have you continued with your inner work, meditation practice, and noted any profound dreams? You've been trained in mindful awareness and your part is to listen carefully for guidance, and follow those subtle directions the best you can. You may be guided during your nighttime dreams, through conversations, or intuition. You may need additional education in the form of a class or courses, like I did.

*** **Education**—I needed to go to college to pursue my guided course of study ... graphics. I also included classes in non-fiction writing, art, and a culinary course over the years. Extensive training was already completed or underway: the holistic healing arts, *A Course in Miracles* ministerial training, entrepreneurial training, and administrative skills.

In the meantime I found other jobs to support me while in college, many of which were helpful to my Ideal Life Path. Remember, there are no accidents. Everything is valid.*

BE BOLD—MAKE A DECISION!

As you read from my personal story, I reviewed my life and all possibilities for a happy future. I made two important decisions: I wanted to make a difference in people's lives and I decided that becoming a writer would be the best possible way for me to do that. Those were my decisions: a goal and a path forward.

Before you finish this chapter and go on to the next one, you MUST have a firm goal and a path forward/solution in mind. If you've aligned yourself with your Higher Power, developed your awareness, and followed your inner wisdom you most likely learned your (outer) life purpose. Your inner life purpose is set by Spirit.

If you don't have a goal and a path forward, then please start over from the beginning. Use the Personal Growth Tools given you, reread and develop your Success Skills, and reread this coaching program. Incorporate the meditations, affirmations, visualizations, and mental rehearsals as much as possible. They're tools that work!

And relax about it. Don't stress out! Surrender to the process, and how happiness is your birthright.

A Tool for Your Personal Growth

You discovered three options from your past: youth and young adult years. You also narrowed down three more options from your present life experiences. Transfer all three to this tool, narrow your options (after your research) and choose one.

1. _____ 2. _____
3. _____ 4. _____
5. _____ 6. _____

Your decision: _____

ACIM says, *"The Power of Decision is your last remaining freedom as a prisoner in this world."* T-12.Vlll.9:1

This is a profound statement about how making wise decisions can lead you to a new Spiritual freedom and away from the limitations of the body and this world.

Everyone Has a Purpose

I mentioned in an earlier chapter that everyone has an outer purpose, and they discover it sometime throughout their lives. It may be revealed in your youth or in middle age. It doesn't matter. It's revealed at the time of its importance. In the meantime, you're on a Spiritual path whether you're aware of it or not.

Whether you think you've learned your life purpose or not, focus on the chapter entitled "Live a Purposeful Life!" This chapter will lead you through a series of exercises to help you construct for yourself and your family a plan for leading a more complete, meaningful, and fulfilling life. Taking these steps will assure you of experiencing a successful and satisfying present and future until your life purpose or Ideal Life Path is revealed to you. You don't want to miss out on all the wonderful experiences that life has to offer. Living a Purposeful Life is designed to make happiness a reality.

Your Next Steps

I can't vouch for where you are in your life, how honest you are with yourself, or your motivation to succeed at birthing a Dream or your Ideal Life Path! I can assure you that once you apply yourself to listening and activating your guidance, your life may never be the same. The Spiritual path can be both subtle and Earth shaking. This is why I continue to ask you to develop your awareness ... so you don't miss out on your transformation or how your Higher Power is working in your life for good.

Keep immersing yourself into your personal growth work. Meet and enjoy other people who are Miracle-minded, metaphysical, or interested in Holistic Health. Continue to read, study, take workshops, and listen to lectures in personal growth and transformation. Participate in guided imagery sessions designed for you to have an inner experience. Your inner experiences always affect your outer experiences.

Your dreams and insights will become more frequent and insightful. I've learned that your transformation could come at any time ... tomorrow, next week, or when you least expect it. All I can say is *"be vigilant about recreating your life and seeing life-changing results!"*

CHAPTER FOURTEEN

THE CHANGING PATH

"Where your attention goes, your energy flows." Unknown author

The goal of the Process of Discovery was to mine your life for clues and details about your sacred seed, leading to the discovery of your Ideal Life Path. You are now stepping onto "The Changing Path." You and your Higher Power are transforming the lost or forgotten you to rebirth the new, more enlightened version of the new you. This is an important chapter for you whether you learned of your destined path or it hasn't been revealed yet.

As someone who is always basically in transition, your path is about to change and it could get bumpy or smooth depending on your decision to follow Guidance. And this is the fork in the road where following Guidance transforms your life from ego-centered to Spirit centered. Will you become a Disciple or just continue to go your own way? Your answer will make all the difference in claiming your soul's purpose.

If you trusted Guidance throughout this program, be ready to listen more deeply for your next steps so you don't make errors or allow your ego to get you off course. If you chose from your ego, you can do what feels right to you. Know that on some level you're still being guided, although not listening to Guidance could slip you up and desired outcomes could take longer than necessary. Several things could happen: your timing may be off. Your unsuitable decisions might cause a detour or something else you need to learn before your Ultimate Opportunity shows up.

You may be one who didn't learn your Ideal Life Path during your process of discovery. Maybe you didn't narrow down your passions from 6 to 3, then to 1. If not, go back and use the Tools for Personal Growth or spend a bit more time reflecting on what's meaningful to you. Please be aware that it may take longer to discover your true path. I've talked about this and it may not be the right time, or there are additional steps to take before you learn your part in your Higher Power's plan for you. It's your Higher Power's plan, not yours or mine. You may have surprising discoveries when you least expect it.

Have you used the Tools for Personal Growth to gain clarity? It's important to be vigilant in answering those questions and in obtaining Guidance. You may have to start over and try again. Trust that where the path leads is the right and perfect path for now.

WHY IS THIS IMPORTANT?

You've discovered your Ideal Life Path ... and that important step is completed. Congratulations! Now it's time to follow your next steps to achieve what is meant to be for you. For anyone who is metaphysical or Miracle-Minded, your dream state, intuition, and inner Guidance are the strongest sources for learning your next steps. Keep in mind that this journey is a process and you are to follow it through as best you can. Be vigilant about accessing your quiet time and noticing synchronicities ... when open doors line up for you.

Clarity Equals Your Turning Point

If you've prepared yourself and connected with your Higher Power at a deep level, you should be ready to move forward with clarity. You can't dally around with your options for years. Because you're focused on this topic at this time in your life, it's most likely the time to make a decision that's meaningful to you. Let it be a Turning Point in your evolution.

Trust that where the path leads is the right and perfect path for now. You should have some idea of where you're going (a Vision) but maybe not the exact directions to get to your destiny. Inner listening is key now! Remember that you're on a specific path now so every bit of Guidance will lead you forward.

*** **Choose Your Path**—Tatiana's parents wanted her to become a medical doctor. She didn't want to go to college for many years to study medicine and basically sacrifice her social and creative life for what her parents wanted. She had other ideas that her parents didn't like. She traveled her own path and attended a trade school. She was talented, successful, and happy with the path she chose.

It was many years later when she fell in love with the idea of becoming a medical doctor. By that time she felt it was too late for her to become a physician. There are times when parents or counselors have your best interests in mind, and you may or may not see it their way. She will never know how a medical career would have played out for her. Sometimes the "idea' of a certain career is better than the actual experience.*

*** **I Did the Opposite**—As a teen, I thought about my options a lot, and decided to follow my parent's lead. Why? I just graduated from high school and rather than work as a laborer in a local steel mill, or struggle financially and risk my independence to pursue my desires, I let it go. I will never know if college at that time in my life would have led me to a better life outcome. I went to the trade school they chose, had a successful career, and an entrepreneurial lifestyle that lasted many years. I traveled, bought a home, and enjoyed a good lifestyle. I wrote business books and inspired many in my industry. It was not until midlife that I was guided to go to college, work part time, and support myself. I believe I was a better student then and I still received a good outcome. *

*** **My Turning Point**—It was early 1990 when I made a decision to become a writer over other options. That decision became a powerful turning point for me. A dream that very night led me in an unexpected direction. I happened to be reading a book in my nighttime dream when I heard someone ask me if I liked it? I replied, *"yes."* That same voice said, *"We're looking for someone to write a book!"* I immediately and enthusiastically said, *"I would do it!"* I felt thrilled to be offered a writing assignment by the Universe so soon after making a commitment to become a writer. This was exciting, to say the least.

Instantly and magically, the book title was written out in front of my minds' eye. The title referred to God. When the dream was over I jumped out of bed and wrote it down. The next morning I remembered the dream and declared, *"I don't know much about God, just what I learned in church sermons, my childhood Sunday school classes, and my metaphysical studies."* I had work to do!*

Assignments are Challenging

Like I mentioned earlier, I take my dreams seriously. I knew this writing assignment would be challenging and I did my best to write the assigned book but I was never happy with the outcome. Looking back on that dream, I don't think the 'writing of a book' was as important as the necessary research to write the book. You'll read how that research evolved and was a stepping-stone to a new life, new experiences, and adventures. Remember, learning your life purpose or Ideal Life Path is most often a process, not a one-stop destination.

That dream and my writing assignment led me to my next step. I studied my Spiritual books stored in my family's garage. The one that made the biggest impact was *A Course in Miracles*. The Workbook Lessons would train me to go to my Higher Power with my life questions and teach me, *"Whatever the question, love is the answer."*

A Course in Miracles is Christian in form but it's content has tones of Eastern thought and Spiritual psychotherapy. Many consider it Jesus' next teaching after the Bible. I personally think of the teaching as Jesus, the Buddha, and Sigmund Freud sitting down together to write a life-changing book for humanity.

The beauty of ACIM is that it's a mind training that first teaches unlearning, and then gives its readers a foundation for inner peace, happiness, forgiveness, and loving relationships. The goal is not to be threatened by what happens in the world, but to forgive it. *("I am not a victim of the world I see."* W-p1.31. ACIM Workbook Lesson.)

"Seek not to change the world, but choose to change your mind about the world." ACIM: Chap 21.

I wondered, *"Was that my real purpose ... to be inspired by and connected to this teaching?"* It turns out that it was an important step in the process. I'll tell you more about how a Big Dream, the ACIM teachings, and my inner Guidance led me to an adventurous life I didn't expect. I committed myself as a writer and I had an assignment from the Universe, so I had work to do!

*** **The Writer's Journey Continues - Stepping Stones**—Leave it to your Higher Power to set up your next step. Little did I know that my decision for the writer's journey would be a life changing turning point for me! Shortly after I decided to become a writer, I found an ad in a Writer's Digest magazine about an I.W.W.G. (International Women's Writing Guild) writer's conference in upstate New York. Past attendees claimed, *"It changed their lives."* I said to myself, *"I'm changing my life, so maybe I should go?"**

I didn't think of it at the time but I was actually nurturing my sacred seed. I was doing so by taking steps toward my Dream of writing to make a difference. The timing was perfect for me to enroll in the writer's conference, book a trip to NYC, and the college in Saratoga Springs. Imagine that!

*** **Revelations!** I had an immediate attraction to the Path of Transformation at the writer's conference, rather than other writing classes. I learned about visualization, guided imagery, forgiveness work, and other aspects of healing the mind and heart. That decision and its resulting experiences sent me on another inner journey.

There were experiences in my meditations and night dreams that revealed what I think of as my Big Dream. It came in the form of a Supernatural Vision while I slept in a college dorm room ... a Grand Vision of what was possible for me, and the world. I realized that all preceding incidents and decisions were steppingstones to this one.

The next morning, as I readied myself for the days' classes, I remembered the Vision/Dream that took me to Northern California for a look at my future. As I went over the whole experience in my mind, I said to myself, *"This venture obviously requires a great deal of money! I think I better win the lottery,"* and chuckled due to the immensity of the project.

During my Vision I hadn't seen any signs or a name on the building. That seemed odd to me. I spoke out loud to myself, *"I didn't see a name on that building!"* In that moment, I completely shocked myself when suddenly the name of that building poured out of my mouth like I actually knew it. Wow! My head was spinning over this epiphany! I wondered, could that Vision be my life purpose and yet I continued to think ... there's got to be more to it than that!

That single experience soon sent me on a journey to Northern California, as guided. I would learn the healing arts, Spiritual content, and the processes that would open minds and hearts. Interested participants would have a heart opening experience and a mindful revelation similar to mine. *

*** **Westward Ho!**—ACIM says, *"A universal theology is impossible, but a universal experience is not only possible, but necessary."* (ACIM: Manual for Teachers, Intro. 2.5.) I returned to Chicago with plans for an inspired life as a writer, and yet ... my Guidance sent me out West ... ASAP!

After moving to San Francisco, I became discouraged with little forward movement and several failures over the years. I eventually experienced more signposts that continued to lead me.*

These personal stories show how quickly things can move when you make decisions from your heart rather than your ego. The skills of patience, faith, and trust got me to places where I didn't know I needed to go. No words can explain the mysteries of life. Once again, for the Miracle- Minded, it's about going with your Guidance and the flow!

SUCCESS SKILLS

Nourishing and nurturing your Sacred Seed is forward motion as you birth your Ideal Life Path into the world. Necessary skills are patience, having faith in the process, and trusting in your part in the Divine plan.

LEARN YOUR LIFE PURPOSE

A Tool for Your Personal Growth

Pay attention to your nighttime dreams. If you remember them upon waking, try to write them down. It's likely some symbols could hold important clues to your future. They could be points, like on a map, to guide you forward to the next signpost.

Take Solid Steps Toward Your Dreams

Solid means, *"Divinely led steps, not ego or absent-minded steps."*

*** **Failure**—When I returned to Chicago from the upstate New York writer's conference, I enrolled in a college writing program. And surprisingly that was not my Guidance. It became very clear that I was to move to Northern California where the Vision occurred ... ASAP!

After becoming trained as a holistic health counselor in San Francisco, I impulsively started my own holistic learning center (in name only). I very quickly realized I had no idea how to operate a holistic center and I didn't have adequate funding. I had been anxious to get a start but not guided to do it, and soon quit as a failed experiment. This is often what happens when one proceeds without hearing Guidance.

Afterward, I took additional courses in the healing arts and opened a private office to practice my craft, which I closed several years later.*

*** **A Major Synchronicity**—While still living in Chicago, my Guidance to become a minister came to me in a nighttime dream. Once I arrived in California I investigated several Theology Schools in Berkeley, but none were a match for my personal and Spiritual belief system. Shortly thereafter, I discovered the only ACIM church in the U.S. at the time. It was near my home. Imagine that! I enrolled in their ministry training and four years later became a legally ordained minister.

Due to my graphics and administrative skills, I was eventually hired at that church/Spiritual center. My previous guidance toward typography and the graphic arts were stepping-stones to acquiring this position.

I received a basic training in how to operate a Spiritual center, but I was not yet guided to take any steps in that direction. I later returned to Omega Institute in New York State where I took a training course on how to *Start a Holistic Healing Center.**

Seek Your North Star!

Think of your desires or Dreams as your North Star that leads you to a better future and more happiness! Even if you know your Ideal Life Path, like I did, be mindful of asking your inner Guide about the next steps to your Dreams before you take them. I feel it's perfectly fine to ponder your Dreams and consider ways they can manifest but don't make yourself crazy with anxiety.

It can be challenging when you're ready to move forward and you don't hear Guidance. You just read my failure experience. I thought I was ready, but had an expensive and disappointing reality check.

There are times when no Guidance is given and intuition doesn't seem to kick in. Intense prayer every single day got me nowhere. It can be frustrating to wait until the next part of the plan is revealed.

*** **Do Your Best**—I can't answer for how your Higher Power sets things up. It has its own timeline and patience is necessary. I didn't waste my time and life waiting around and doing nothing. As you've read from my many stories, I worked lots of dead end jobs and part time gigs. I worked in kitchens, catering, conferences, cooking school, offices, retirement homes, and salons over the years. After not receiving Guidance on starting a Holistic Center, I started pursued the careers on my original wish list (artist, writer, and culinary expert/cooking school teacher) and temporarily returned to an old career. I took consistent action and eventually accomplished all my goals, except the Big Dream.

I continued to be active in my Spiritual community, giving sermons, teaching classes, and helping with conferences. I attended many personal growth conferences and seminars. Writing transformative books is a constant activity. Being Miracle-Minded inspires me to continuously add to my skill set for my Big Dream.

The important thing to note here is that I didn't receive guidance NOT to accomplish other goals. It felt right and the rent had to be paid.*

North Star Tips

Be mindful of asking your inner Guide about your next steps before you take them. If you don't hear anything, look back at your findings from The Process of Discovery. Take necessary steps toward your Dreams to prove your intentions.

Do you dream of becoming an actor? Take acting classes, read books about acting, or join a local Playhouse where you can receive experience. Your intentions might inspire Guidance.

Metaphysical thought says you can't make a mistake and there are no accidents. Keep asking questions in your meditations to discover answers. Keep taking steps and pursuing your Spirit-inspired goals.

Think of your desires or Dreams as your North Star! Notice if they lead you in a particular direction toward happiness. That's what it's all about, isn't it? ... HAPPINESS NOW!

If you aren't receiving Guidance, take a look at what does inspire you, appeal to you, or speak to you. Choose a career that speaks to your heart.

You can work various jobs while getting necessary experience for your Dream. You never know who you'll meet or what opportunities show up.

*** **On Purpose**—I've had other experiences you need to hear. I've made important decisions resulting in actions where I didn't feel like I received guidance. My life was upended during the 2020 pandemic so I temporarily traveled to Mexico until plan A was approved. It was only after I arrived there when I realized I was called there "on purpose," an experiment to learn about retiring South of the border, a long held Dream of mine.*

When situations align you can assume that your intuition was at play, and take steps toward what you need to do. You'll discover later that your actions are perfect. That's not always the case, but when doors open, that's a sign you're going in the right direction. The Universe is supporting you.

SUCCESS SKILLS

The success skill for this solution is to continue listening to your heart and your guidance the best you can. If you are on the right track there should be no difference between your Dream, the Spirit-inspired goals of your heart, and the direction of your Guidance.

A Tool for Your Personal Growth

What steps can you take today toward your Dreams or Ideal Life Path? Can you interview a VIP, take a course, learn how to use a computer, write your memoir, or talk with people you trust about your discoveries?

Look for Signposts to Stay on Course

You've most likely driven on long stretches of road with no markers or road signs. Anxiety sometimes sets in when you're unsure if you're on the right path. A road sign or highway marker can help you gain confidence and direction.

The same situation applies to following your Dream or waiting for directions to your Ideal Life Path. It can be tempting to reverse course or become doubtful and lose faith when you don't experience some kind of sign. When you're on a certain course that you believe in ... keep looking for the signs, synchronicities, and open doors.

*** **Unexpected Messages**—Unexpected signposts are always a surprising and welcome gift. I met a friendly young woman at my first extensive hypnotherapy training in Northern California. As we spoke, she reported that she knew a very good psychic in her Southern home state. Her psychic told her that, when in California, she would meet a woman named Linda. Since I was the only Linda in the class, she approached me.

During one of our conversations she gave me a more definitive message regarding my own Spiritual Vision. I had not previously disclosed it to her. Her message was so 'right on' that my mouth dropped ... literally! Her Southern psychic revealed the name of my Vision given to me in Upstate New York. It was a perfect example of the One Mind experience when he psychic tapped into the Universal Mind.

I don't typically visit psychics, so this was a revelation to me. This good news became a powerful signpost that kept my Big Dream alive in my mind and heart at a time when it was faltering.*

Signposts to Your Ideal Life Path

Spirit-inspired Visions or Big Dreams do not happen everyday. A synchronistic signpost may not come directly to you ... but through people you randomly meet. There could be a time span of many years from the time you have the Vision, Dream, or Calling to the time it is made manifest in the world.

It's comforting to get a sign or see a signpost every so often. Why? It's so easy to become doubtful. A Vision or Dream is a Spiritual experience that isn't real to others, but only to you. Because of that, you need to keep that sacred seed alive within yourself ... your heart and mind. Have faith, because your Ideal Life Path is part of your Higher Power's plan and because of that, you must keep taking steps forward as guided. Follow the Guidance you do get even if it appears to take you in a different direction. My graphic arts degree got me an important office position.

Less than a year after my Vision in upstate New York, I hired an architectural renderer to create a life-like drawing of what I experienced. I knew it would take a long time to manifest and I didn't want to forget it. I look at it from time to time to keep myself motivated.

Know that you're still on purpose ... whatever you're doing now. Maybe there's something that you need, some kind of experience? You most likely still have some personal growth work to do on yourself, connections to make, or lessons to learn. Remember, the Universe works in its own time ... not yours.

People who succeed in all walks of life claim they were persistent and didn't give up. Use that advice to build up your confidence and expand your skills, if necessary.

SUCCESS SKILLS

The skills needed for this step are patience, mindfulness, and the awareness to stay in the present moment. Observe where you're at, what you're doing, and how it applies to your Dream. Take notice of the people you meet. There may be important synchronicities. Someone may have important things to say or be someone who can open doors for you. Stay centered with your Dream and don't be too surprised when signs or clues show up.

*** **Supernatural Lovelies**—Synchronicities to me, are supernatural lovelies. Not long ago, my goal was to create a specific new meditation course to teach online and in person. During my research I discovered a type of meditation called Yoga Nidra, which is NOT like yoga.

Yoga is an effective Spiritual practice used for stretching the body in ways to have it be flexible and healthy. Yoga Nidra, also called *yogic sleep*, is for stretching the mind and its awareness. Since I had an extensive background in guided imagery, I thought it would be a perfect fit for me. So I studied Yoga Nidra, upgraded my meditation knowledge and credential, and included an Art Therapy training.

Due to synchronicity, at the exact same time I completed my additional meditation training I discovered a new online course. It was perfect ... "How to Create Your Own Self-knowledge Online Course." Imagine that!

Many years ago I tried to create an educational course with no success. This time I knew who the trainers were but the training was considerably more expensive and much more detailed. After the free preliminary training, I needed to make a decision to enroll or not. Based on the synchronistic timing, and the teacher's well-known reputation, I impulsively decided to take the leap and sign up for the training. Because of my commitment to create an online meditation course and its potential to escalate my teaching of Miracle-Mindedness, a miracle occurred! Yes, a supernatural lovely!

Early the next morning (after paying for the course and making the commitment the previous night) my inner Guide awoke me with a new title and the initial information for my new course, *"Learn Your Life Purpose!"* I saw this exciting moment as a road sign and stepping stone on the way to my Big Dream and life purpose. And you've probably noticed how much important meditation and mindfulness instruction is included in this coaching program? It's Key!*

Where are the Road Signs?

When you are on the right path, you will experience road signs. Start adding them up. One sign can be somewhat meaningful, whereas a number of them have substance and can offer something more poignant.

You're sure you're on the right path but see no road signs? That's okay too. Where you are is the right and perfect place for you. Remember, there are no accidents! Stay in the present moment with whatever you're learning, and keep your mind and heart focused on where you're going. Be patient and enjoy where you are.

There's a possibility that what you're learning now will be valuable later, just like my graphic arts, holistic health, and entrepreneurial trainings were to my Ideal Life Path.

The potential challenge here is continuing to take trainings but never do anything with them. Education is valuable and when you're learning with a goal in mind ... use it or you lose it.

Maybe you want something different to happen but your world is not changing? That could mean the Universe i.e. your Higher Power, doesn't have a change for you in this now moment.

Perhaps your Ideal Life Path is calling you, but you're experiencing some level of doubt or fear. You find it intimidating to step ahead on your path. I've hit that roadblock myself ... many times! That's okay! Just keep moving forward, doing what you can. Take a class to build your confidence or whatever you need to do to overcome your fear. Try listening to your creative intuition: ask, visualize, and affirm.

A Tool for Your Personal Growth

You're on a roll now so the next time you pray or meditate ask your Higher Power for a sign, especially if you're feeling uncomfortable with your direction. Use your prayer time (for asking) and meditation time (to listen), and always remember to be patient.

Your Next Steps

Your Dream or Ideal Life Path may be right around the corner or some years into the future. I learned of my Ideal Life Path when I was in my mid forties. I was in the process of ending one of my former Dreams from high school—business ownership. So please don't give up or fret if you aren't aware of it yet! Realize that you are on a constantly changing path and there will be bumps, twists, and turns on your way to doing your Higher Powers' will. In the meantime, do what you love and enjoy your life!

Be mindful of turning points, synchronicities, and signposts. Noticing them will help to keep you in a positive or hopeful state. In the meantime ... enjoy your life and don't worry about the small stuff. As best-selling author Richard Carlson always said, *"Don't worry about the small stuff ... It's all small stuff!"*

CHAPTER FIFTEEN

LIVE YOUR PURPOSEFUL LIFE

"A Dream written down with a date becomes a goal, a goal broken down into steps becomes a plan, a plan backed by action becomes a reality!" Unknown

The popular shoe manufacturer Nike says, *"Just do it!"* Its iconic athletic brand is just as well known for their logo: a stylistic checkmark and inspirational moniker, as for their top of the line sports shoes and apparel. According to their website, Nike's brand is founded upon the Biblical word, nikao, which means to overcome or to rule.

* **Just Do It!**—Long before Christianity, there was the winged Greek goddess, Nike, who brought the message of speed and victory! Nike's focused brand alludes to the idea that everyone may potentially overcome hurdles. You could sum up the idea behind it with just three words, JUST DO IT! And an associated check mark that says, *"It's done!"* The message, as I understand it is: *"Buy and wear our shoes so you can quickly walk, run, or jump into your goals and achieve your Dreams. Our shoes will support you, help you in your efforts to fly/soar into your amazing future."*

Nike says*, "Our purpose is to move the world forward through the power of sport."* We know they achieve more than that … to champion victory! Brilliant!*

There was a time, pre-Christianity, when people believed in and worshipped Roman and Greek gods and goddesses for their gifts of strength, victory, and wisdom. Today we believe that our strength comes from our belief in our Higher Power, inner Guides, Jesus/Jeshua, the Buddha, and other God's of the heart. The Miracle-Minded believe in the Oneness of all things, looking inward for Guidance to achieve your life purpose.

You've learned a lot about going inward for strength to overcome your challenges and burdens, but also for goal achievement. This chapter and coaching is designed to help you to "Just Do It!" Discover the strength and purpose within your Self!" It's there! Every time you doubt yourself, remember the popular bumper sticker that says, *"Don't believe everything you think!"*

WHY IS THIS IMPORTANT?

The purpose of this chapter is to give you the important tools for living a "purposeful life" whether you have or haven't learned of your Ideal Life Path or Life Purpose. This present moment is precious time. Life is short so lets make every precious moment count toward your happiness. I promise you that your time and effort is not wasted. The spontaneous actions you intuitively take today will pay off when you learn of your life purpose and then say to yourself, "I was led to this all along!"

Be Confident—Move Forward

As you learned from the shoe manufacturer, Nike, *moving forward* is a valuable and worthwhile purpose. Did you take action and get valuable insights while reading The Process of Discovery and The Changing Path? If you didn't uncover your sacred seed, perhaps you weren't as focused as you could be? Maybe it's just not your time to learn of your Ideal Life Path and that's okay! Don't worry about it ... enjoy your life and know that the joy, love, and light you share is also your purpose!

The Miracle-Minded know you're meant to reach your fullest potential and being on purpose is to take confident movement forward, even if its baby steps ... just do it!

When you answered the questions in The Process of Discovery, you had to come up with something! If anything exciting or significant jumped out at you, take an action toward manifesting it to see if it leads you closer to your desires. That past desire may just be a fantasy and that's okay. Just go with it if it seems sticky and has any meaning for you.

A purposeful life starts with a desire, a plan, and actions. You'll achieve a meaningful and fulfilling life more quickly and thoughtfully by creating a focused plan for a purposeful life.

*** Be Purposeful!—When my Big Dream was revealed to me, I said to myself, *"Wow, that's awesome but there's no way I have the money or expertise to pull this off!"* My emotions were both positive and negative at the same time. Ugh! I knew it was going to take time and additional training. And that's exactly what happened.

To accomplish anything in life: buy a house, find a romantic partner, or learn a new language, you'll need to be purposeful with your actions. Create a goals' strategy or plan, be flexible and persistent, and keep a positive mindset. This chapter is all about following in Nike's footsteps ... moving forward with any Dream or goal you may be nurturing and taking steps to realize the amazing future you deserve.*

Remember Your Wise Internal Resources

You may not have been born with the same advantages in life as another individual, but you have the same wise internal Resources to draw upon. That truth is powerful and unchangeable. Your internal and eternal Resource, your Higher Power, doesn't have biases or prejudices to hold you back. In fact, It loves you beyond measure and plans only for your happiness. Your Higher Power provides all the means, gifts, and Resources to help you along in your life. I can't think of any area where your wise inner Resource can't help you through your struggles. Whether it's your career, relationships, or direction in life, the Universe has your back. Above all, you must go with the flow and not fight it. I've experienced that truth for myself and from individuals I've interviewed.

I can't answer for how you're processing this program and its success in your life at this point. The first few chapters were designed to upgrade your mindset. Then you were encouraged to upgrade your communication with your Higher Power. You spent a bit more time in prayer, meditation, and reflecting on how you could be of service to the world and give of your gifts and talents. You constantly processed your answers from the Tools for Personal Growth. If you participated in the program designed for you, then you are in a good place to become a purposeful person.

To find meaning and joy in Living Your Purposeful Life diminishes the possibility of having regrets later in life. You may remember my story, "My Day to Die" and the wish I made and how I handled it from that day forward.

Mindfully moving forward brings about a lifetime of conscious and fulfilling experiences. Do your best to bring about positive situations for yourself and those who depend on you. Bring an element of faith and trust to every circumstance and relationship. Confirm your purposeful intentions now and experience more joy and satisfaction in your future!

What I'm asking you to do in this chapter is to get right with your life, prepare and plan for your most meaningful, joyful, and fulfilling experiences. Involve your right mind, your heart, and your inner Resources.

Goals as a Roadmap to a Purposeful Life

I invite you to be clear and focused about your values and personal/professional goals. Those two important areas could give you clarity on where to place your focused energy. The following story about Jeremy demonstrates how you can achieve your desires with a plan and a bit of patience and persistence. There's a popular quote by John Lennon, a famous musician with the former Beatles. He said, *"Life is what happens while you're making other plans."*

*** **Goals**—Jeremy is an excellent example of someone who lives a purposeful life, plans his life according to his passions, and lives his truths, regardless of any setbacks. You can do the same with your own purposeful life, according to your passions and persistence.

At a young age he tuned into the future he wanted to live and created a life plan to make it happen. He was interested in science in high school and one Christmas he asked for the gift of a science kit. He was often observed in his room, looking through his microscope at various specimens. No one knew where that would eventually lead, except for Jeremy. He knew!

Jeremy went to college and became a clinician/scientist who studies the structure, function, and behavior of cells. It's used to diagnose or screen for cancer. He worked his entire life in that field. Jeremy married a nurse at around 30 years of age, as planned, and they had the three children they agreed upon.

Throughout his life he and his wife planned to retire and live in a warm climate. About ten years before his retirement, they bought a nice vacation home in a foreign country and used it regularly. After his wife unexpectedly passed away just before her retirement, Jeremy didn't want to be alone, but to share his retired life with a beloved companion. A couple of years later he met a lovely woman whom he planned to marry in a year. A year later they became a happily married couple and traveled the world according to their plan.*

On Becoming Purposeful

There was an Oprah Winfrey interview on YouTube of the well-known author and medical intuitive, Carolyn Myss. When Oprah asked her specifically about purpose, Myss replied, *"If you're alive, you have a purpose."*

Everything you do and every undertaking is a purposeful step toward some lesser or more important goal. Whether your goal is to plant a garden in your backyard or build an empire, it takes purposeful steps. You can't NOT be on purpose, but you may not always see it as such. Remember that your every *inaction* is also an action and counts toward or away from your goal. Even procrastination can work against you. Remember that every small purposeful step you take could possibly have a positive or negative effect on someone else's purpose.

You've learned through your religious or Spiritual studies that 'God has a plan for everyone.' Allow it to reveal itself naturally and not through struggle. The Miracle-Minded find through one's life experiences that only your Higher Power's plan or will for your happiness will work.

*** Failure—Remember when I said my first effort to start a holistic center failed? I learned several important lessons from that experience, mostly about waiting for guidance before I act. That's okay because I'm always willing to pursue a goal for the value of its experience, even if I don't achieve the goal at that point in time. At least I know where not to go or what not to do! I realized, *"I can do better!"**

ACIM has a valuable workbook lesson that can be repeated often, *"All things are lessons God would have me learn."* (ACIM: W-193)

SUCCESS SKILLS

In order to create a purposeful life, you'll need the skills of *mindfulness* to zero in on the life or lifestyle you desire. You'll need the skill of clarity, persistence, and most likely patience. And then there are the skills of *making a decision and following through.*

The Power of Your Personal Values

Your personal values are the powerful principles, beliefs, and ethical standards that guide your behavior and decision-making. They represent what is important to you and what you consider to be morally and socially acceptable. Personal values are deeply ingrained, can influence how you perceive the world, interact with others, and choose a life path.

Personal values that may apply to you:

Honesty: Your commitment to truthfulness, transparency, and sincerity in your actions.

Integrity: Adherence to a strong moral and ethical code. It often involves consistency in your values and behavior.

Respect: This is about treating others with consideration, dignity, and regard for their feelings, rights, and boundaries.

Compassion: Compassion is a powerful demonstration of empathy and kindness toward others, especially in times of need or suffering.

Loyalty: This value is about being steadfast and faithful in your relationships, commitments, and responsibilities.

Ambition: Your strong drive to achieve personal and professional goals.

Creativity: You value innovative thinking and expression in various forms, including art, problem-solving, and entrepreneurship.

Spirituality or Religion: Your personal beliefs in a Higher Power or a faith tradition.

Adventurousness: You seek new experiences, challenges, and personal growth.

Education: The importance of continuous learning, knowledge, and personal growth.

Health/Wellness: You prioritize physical and mental well-being and a healthy lifestyle.

Open-Mindedness: You have a willingness to consider different perspectives and adapt to new information or experiences.

Gratitude: You acknowledge and appreciate the positive aspects of life and the contributions of others.

Personal values play a significant role in shaping your identity, influencing your priorities, and guiding your decision-making in all aspects of life. Your values may evolve over time and may be influenced by cultural, societal, and personal experiences. Understanding your personal values is important for making meaningful life choices and building a sense of purpose and fulfillment.

A Tool for Your Personal Growth

Think about what you value. Read the list above to establish your values. You might share this exercise with your romantic partner and with your children. Write your values here:

1.
2.
3.
4.
5.

Brainstorm Your Way to Happiness Now

Living a Purposeful Life is easier to pursue once you (and your mate/partner and children etc.) sit down with your thoughts, your Dream or desires, a pen and paper. This brainstorming step should ideally be done before marriage or a partnership and again later … perhaps every few years or when big changes are happening to either one of you. You're essentially planning for your potential happiness, and that's important!

If you desired to start a new business, you would sit down and create a business plan so you have clarity on the particulars and direction of your business. You could follow the same idea for your present and future life like Jeremy did in his previous story, "Goals." Of course you must also assume that something will change, like a divorce or death, and the plan must change along with extenuating circumstances. But what if you won the lottery, inherited money or a vacation home, or if your new business failed? You'll need to go with the flow and change direction. Plans are not written in stone.

You may think of a purposeful life as the values and sometimes material parts of life that are personally important to you: marriage to a compatible partner, a home in a good neighborhood, a savings account and investments, raising your children with good moral values and education, regular vacation time with loved ones or other meaningful desires.

Think through what will bring feelings of happiness or satisfaction. Maybe it's not a new car every few years, but a longer or more interesting vacation. Instead of time on the beach, you may desire a learning experience or to help build a new home for the homeless.

Brainstorm and make a list. Starting small with some simple goals will help you take on larger goals over time. Feel free to make changes. Taking small or large action steps to accomplish your desires more quickly could lead you to achieve a larger Dream. There are formulas for you to follow and I'll provide some for you.

You can make all kinds of plans and they can manifest for you when you provide some level of clarity on your future so it's productive, fulfilling, and joyful. I don't think you want your future to repeat itself and become like the past? You'll miss out on all the interesting or surprising gifts the Universe has in store for you.

Whichever way it goes, it has to be okay for you whether you achieve everything in your purposeful life or not. Don't stress out about anything. Go with the flow and follow your roadmap the best you can and be open to surprises! The Universe is full of surprises, so let go and enjoy the ride!

An Exercise in Living Your Best Life

This particular process is mostly for single individuals who desire a Spiritual slant to his/her life. The process of creating a purposeful life is about thinking through or dreaming up, preferably with guidance, the kind of life that brings you joy. Allow it to be an exercise in living your best life. Make it compelling, exciting, adventurous or however you want to live. Be creative and see where it goes.

Step 1. Applying your conscious intention, write down your current goals.

Step 2. Close your eyes and in your minds' eye create the most compatible co-worker/employer situation, personal relationship, or creative expression that could ever enhance your life.

Step 3. Allow your subconscious mind, through your quiet mental time, to activate and integrate your focused requests so the Universe can help you achieve them.

Step 4. Be optimistic and patient! Know that the Universe is subtly leading you to your joy. Don't fight it by trying to control the situation! Keep your focus and meditate on or imagine the various pleasing aspects of your goals ... whether you already know your path or not.

Step 5. Dream BIG but write down your ideas for small steps that you could take each day. Baby steps are the less stressful way to get to your BIG destination.

Step 6. Do a mental rehearsal to see and feel yourself experiencing your goals or desires.

* You may want to do a mental rehearsal right before bedtime, so you go to sleep with a positive intention. Remember what I said in an earlier chapter ... your will is the same as your Higher Power's will. *"The script is written."* (ACIM) Your destiny is implanted within your sacred seed. It means you and your Higher Power are in cahoots on this and it's up to you to follow your inner Guidance to nourish and nurture that seed.

A Purposeful Plan Creates A Purposeful Life

To layout a plan or blueprint for your life is an excellent exercise in imagination and purpose. It's not that difficult nor is it always easy. It's plain and simple: You choose it, you plan it, and you take action! Does it happen the way you plan? It's possible but not always and I'll talk about why!

To lead a purposeful life is to do it with intention. It's a well thought out process where your chosen career, family life, vacations, retirement, and your relationships are aligned with the purpose you assigned to them. That means everything in alignment with your values and personal goals is the most direct path to your Happiness Now experience!

Success in each area is due to thoughtful decision-making, planning, and execution. It's not about living life haphazardly or by the seat of your pants. (Although impulsive actions and situations can be fun and rewarding. Don't miss out on these!) Start making a list of 25-50 (or more) things you want to do or achieve in your life.

Everything you do has a purpose otherwise you wouldn't be doing it. What specific purpose would actions on your list achieve? For example, you heard that a favorite personal empowerment speaker is part of a week-long event in a desirable location you've always wanted to explore. Make a plan where you can work backwards from your end point. Your desire is to attend a wintertime personal growth retreat in a sunny and warm climate. It's now June. Working backward, you would:

1) Research various retreats that occur in a warm climate and include your favorite speaker.

2) Make contact with several retreat centers to discover their cost, location, amenities, theme, menu, speakers, transportation, and other requirements.

3) You choose from the available retreat dates, pay a deposit, and choose an airline if necessary.

4) Make necessary payments from your financial account to the retreat company as addressed in their contract.

5) Confirm your trip, pack your bags, and enjoy your retreat.

6) Make your plan yearly or in three to five-year increments.

* Think of my suggestions like a buffet. Use the ideas you like and leave the rest. There's no harm in doing that. You may possibly change your mind and come back later to absorb and integrate the ideas you originally bypassed.

Your Template for a Purposeful Life

I've listed seven steps that I believe could help you achieve your more detailed goals. If they're Spirit-inspired goals—so much the better!

Step #1: The first step to leading a purposeful life is to decide what kind of life you want to live, and then go into detail: single, married, children, no children, religious, spiritual, or atheist etc., highly educated or moderately educated, career position, hobbies, location (in the U.S. or abroad?), home ownership or rental, travel, or any of the other options you find attractive. Be open to every option.

Step #2: The second step is to create a list of more defined goals you want to achieve—according to your choices in Step #1. Narrow them down as best you can. Example: What kind of business? What niche? What location? What target market? Employees: age, training, etc.?

Step #3: Set a timeline for each goal. Be specific, right down to the details of every aspect of your life: by what age you'll be married, how many children you'll have, how you'll earn your living, where you and your family vacation, what neighborhood you'll live in and other details.

Step #4: Use your time management skills to stay in synch with what you want to accomplish.

Step #5: Take action steps. Write out the steps that you believe would help you reach your goals.

Step #6: Make your decisions at the appropriate times throughout your life.

Step #7: Review your goals every three to five years. Understand that this is the world of change and you can expect the unexpected. Things, thoughts, and intentions will change. Be ready to go with the flow!

* Remember that as you write or speak these goals, the Universe hears every word so be certain you mean what you say. Choices from your ego are unlikely to materialize.

A Tool for Your Personal Growth

Create your personal mind map. Take all the information you've gathered thus far and make a one page mind map. Draw a circle in the middle of the page. Start with your Dream, Big Dream (s), or even a desirable and focused fantasy. Nothing is off limits especially if it feels intuitively correct to you.

Start your brainstorming session and begin writing your ideas or steps on the page. Include everything that comes to your mind. You can always adjust it later. When you run out of ideas, connect the areas that are similar and create your intentional goal-directed strategy or roadmap. Set it up so every decision is made with intention and as a means for accomplishing your purposeful life. In other words, also include action steps and a timeline with each goal.

Create Life Goals for a Purposeful Life

I've made it a big deal in this program to always ask for guidance about any decision. That's always the first thing to do. If you don't get an answer, don't feel frustrated. Take a bit of time to wait for an answer and search your heart.

*** **Pray**—I felt it necessary to jump ahead, do the research, and get a feeling for what I thought suited me. I prayed my decision was in alignment with my Higher Power's will. Sometimes I missed the mark and other times I hit a bulls' eye! The previous solutions may help you through the traditional ways of setting goals.*

Aim for Your Target and Be Magnetic

A goal is an aim or a purpose. Life goals are what you want to achieve now or in the near or distant future. They're much more meaningful than just what you need to accomplish in order to survive. Unlike daily routines or short-term objectives, they drive your behaviors over the long run.

Accomplish your goals through strategic steps. Do research on how much education, finances, or time you need to achieve each specific goal. Desiring to start a business is very different from desiring a romantic relationship. You may or may not require a nicer wardrobe, more personal grooming, or an upgrade of social skills.

There are a number of ways to manifest a romantic relationship: read recommended books on the subject, ask friends to introduce you to single people, join a dating service, or frequent places where you'll find like-minded people. Example: If you enjoy sailing, join a yacht club. If you enjoy playing cards, racing cars, or playing golf, go to places where those activities draw people like you. As always ... let your Higher Power know you've worked on yourself and you're ready! This last tactic worked for me.

To attract the right and perfect relationship, be the person who you want to be with and who also wants to be with you! You might start out by making a list of the qualities and values you desire. Then take a look at the list to notice if the qualities are present in you? Be magnetic!

Take AIM at what you want or where you're going. Is it a new car, a higher degree, a larger home, a more active social life, or a more robust retirement plan? Strategize through research and preparations.

The instant you think of a goal, write it down so you don't forget. Put your journal in a place where you can see it everyday and update it. Be purposeful about the goals that can make your life more enriching, fun, altruistic, or meaningful, and develop your plan with intention. Take action as often as possible.

Goals for the Five Major Areas of Life

Thee are traditional ways to track your goals. Your goals can be handled in one or two ways and both are right. The first is the traditional way: use the Five Standard Life Goals: career, financial, personal development, spiritual, and relationship.

The other way is to be led by your Higher Power, which will always take you to your heart's desire. Start with these five goals and take your answers into your next meditation. Sometimes your inner Guide will make corrections by suggesting something else or deleting an idea.

Remember my story of when my Higher Power changed the title of my potential online meditation course to *"Learn Your Life Purpose?"* Father knows best!

1. Career Goals: *"Where do you see yourself in 5 years, 10 years, 15 years?"* Vividly visualize each stage in your development. Be clear about what you want, and how you'll align your Dreams with your inner Guidance. Celebrate your victories in all the areas below.

2. Financial Goals: *"What investments will you make: home, vacation home, car or truck, recreation vehicle, retirement savings, or yourself!"* Set goals for each one. This is the most expedient way to get what you want. Ask the Universe to support you and reveal your Storehouse.

3. Personal Development Goals: *"What additional education will you attain?"* Explore the possibilities to help you be the best version of yourself. Also be open to the potential that is already within you. How can you show your light and extend your inner wisdom?

4. Spiritual Goals: *"What church, temple, or Spiritual center will you attend?"* Will you tithe to support your Spiritual community? How will you contribute to your Spiritual development and community? How will you receive Spiritual gifts from your commitment?

5. Relationship Goals: *"What will you do to achieve a happy intimate relationship, or a balanced relationship with friends, family, co-workers, or neighbors?"* How will you share your light, love, and laughter?

A Tool for Your Personal Growth

Read through your goals and write your first ideas for each one in your journal or here.

1.
2.
3.
4
5.

Food for Thought

Your situation is your situation, and your skills and background may or may not be suitable right now for your Ideal Life Path. Since your Ideal Life Path is specialized for you and your souls' purpose, just know that you'll be groomed or are possibly already being groomed for the part you'll play to co-create your life and your Higher Power's will for your soul.

Many metaphysically minded people believe they came to Earth with an assignment or a situation that needed to be healed. Those who are aware of their assignments attempt to achieve them like I have. Others feel they agreed to something they no longer want to honor ... and it might be detrimental to their growth. They want to break their contract with an assignment for personal reasons. I've helped clients break their contract with chronic abusive relationships and negative situations that never appeared to get better or heal. They feel free of that burden and are able to move on.

Remember, your Ideal Life Path is not necessarily about you, per se. It's about your soul and its purpose here. It's about your higher Self that is always Spiritually connected to your Higher Power.

How Guidance Works

Your Higher Power or inner Guide communicates directions to your conscious, subconscious, or super-conscious mind. Your mind hears those words/ideas and communicates them to your awareness either directly as an inner Voice or through ESP (Extra Sensory Perception). Next, you have thoughts and perceptions, perhaps resulting in judgments about what you received. You may or may not judge those thoughts, but from there you make one of three decisions: to receive and act, ignore, or hold for later.

To the Miracle-Minded your body is the communication device between your Higher Power and you, and also between your thoughts/perceptions and the health of your body. Just like the food you eat affects your body, so do the thoughts you think on a daily basis—especially the negative ones.

Move through any fear of failure, imposter syndrome, or financial instability by remembering how badly you want Happiness Now! You are now getting clear on taking steps to Live a Purposeful Life whether your Ideal Life Path is revealed to you right now or not. Just because you haven't learned of it yet doesn't mean it's not on its way to you. If you have any inkling of what's in store for you, start preparing for it now!

*** **Stay Strong!**—That's what I did … stay strong through the preparation stages! I took about four years of training in the Healing Arts, Holistic Health, *A Course in Miracles,* and writing/art classes to be prepared for my Ideal Life Path. None of the trainings were a burden. I undertook them with joy and promise. Give it time to come together for you.*

Your Next Steps

You've been given various options or a roadmap for achieving whatever goals, Dreams, or desires appeal to you. Look at your list or plan and determine how you feel about it on a scale of one to ten.

Give yourself a reality check and determine if your list is complete or lacking in some way. Could it be more exciting, adventurous, conservative, or free-spirited? If you're not excited about it, then you might need a do-over until you get to the point of confidence in your plan and confidence in yourself to achieve your goals.

Try not to stress out about it … just know that your Higher Power's plan for you will always manifest. Just don't put up roadblocks!

In the next and final chapter, you'll explore the most important areas regarding your Ideal Life Path. You'll uncover the more intimate parts of your life that are significant to your soul's journey and achievements. If it's important to you to accomplish your Soul's Purpose, you'll learn about the aspects beyond materialism: love, harmony in relationships, forgiveness, peace of mind, personal growth, and spiritual healing, etc. These are the areas that matter to the soul.

CHAPTER SIXTEEN

READJUST YOUR HALO

"Singing a song of love in your own heart reverberates in the hearts of others." –
Linda L. Chappo

Chapter One started with a dialogue about defying the statistics, which state that many people, like you, either don't love your work or can't stand your co-workers or managers. You eventually continue your search for another position, career, or team more to your liking. This typically does not happen if you are experiencing happiness while living your Ideal Life Path. My sense of it is that when you readjust your halo, that intention replaces the clouds hanging over your head with a beautiful circular rainbow instead.

As I've said before, *A Course in Miracles* is a mind-training. It trains you to correct your misperceptions and to focus on the will of your Higher Power and the awareness of your Spiritual unfolding. You're slowly loosening your misperceptions until you awaken to a higher reality. *The higher reality is a greater awareness of the love that exists.*

These shifts in your perceptions lead to greater peace and happiness through accepting these two goals set by the Miracle-Minded: your Higher Power as first in your life and secondly, right-minding your relationships. That's what you want, right? You can't have the ultimate peace and happiness unless your relationships are a reflection of that desire. The intention of this final chapter is to give you more clarity on how to make that important shift.

The Miracle-Minded know if you're guided to move on, or feel the energy that tells you to do something different, then there is something better waiting for you. The idea is to be aligned with your Higher Power's will for you. It may not always be necessary to move to another career or end a relationship but instead … readjust your halo.

I said earlier that you are a Spiritual being in a human body and are having a personal growth experience. Your body and its bossy ego isn't necessarily aware of its soul's Spiritual perfection. The goal of Spiritual awareness is to bring that truth to light. According to the Miracle-Minded, it's accomplished through the awareness, gratitude, and light of your personal relationships. If your relationships aren't peaceful, you'll need to reach inward and make some adjustments to your dark side, the shadow that stands behind your light!

If you quit your job, career, or industry due to difficult interpersonal relationships, you may have left unhealed relationships in your wake. This means it's time to readjust your halo. The Miracle-Minded know that, to your Higher Power, you (as your Spiritual identity) are innocent. But your ego self is usually misguided and when it is, your less than admirable behavior is *a call for love*. And if no one is answering that call … you've got a people problem. So, in other words, you have some mental and emotional housecleaning and corrections to take care of.

I'll cut right to the chase … your ultimate purpose as someone who is Miracle-Minded is to bring an element of forgiveness to yourself, your relationships, and the world. Therein lies your happiness.

Without forgiveness, you've limited your ability to achieve true and lasting happiness and peace! Allow me to be blunt. There's no peace when you haven't forgiven yourself or your relationships for any indiscretions. It doesn't matter whether you're the perceived villain or someone else is. Spiritually, you're responsible for your own attitude.

If you think you're free of that person or people by quitting your job or moving away, think again. You're not free of them. If there's bad energy between you: if the thought of him/her haunt you, you are mentally, emotionally, and psychically chained to that person. You'll sense negative energies hanging onto your coattails until you heal those wounds and forgive them. When you can bring that person/people to memory and have no ill thoughts … the chains are broken.

WHY IS THIS IMPORTANT?

It's pretty difficult to achieve your purpose unless you learn to get along with people. You really do need each other but you may not love each other. It's important to reassess or look at your relationships differently and to heal them … if you're emotionally mature and willing. Healing and forgiving another is easier said than done, especially if you're stuck in your anger and you have a need to be right.

You're Not a Victim

You can determine who is the victim (in your perception), how you or others got to that status, and how it can be shifted to a better place. I've said many times that you are not a victim! To readjust your halo means you'll both benefit from getting clarity and shifting your perceptions ... that God deems you both innocent. Mirroring explains that.

I'm clear that you can't like/love everyone or even see eye-to-eye. What you can do is let the negative energy go because it doesn't serve anyone. Don't dwell on it, but do your best to free each other from anger or hatred ... then move on. Try, to the best of your ability, to *understand the call for love*. What was that person really after?

You simply can't have a successful level of relationship happiness unless you transition from loveless or fear-based thinking to love-based thinking. Learn how, with a little willingness, it can change your life and the lives of those you interact with.

We talked about you as a Spirit having a human experience. You're Spirit first, and a human second. Because you're a Spirit first it's radically important that you serve your soul, or your Spiritual existence. It's the higher, more authentic, more loving, considerate, and genuine aspect of you. Once you're connected, in alignment, and co-creating with your Higher Power, you'll have the Miracle-Minded consciousness to get your relationships and overall life into a fabulous place.

Part One: Be Miracle-Minded for Yourself

Show Up as Your Best Self!

The one area where you either shine or go dark is how you show up in the world. Your attitude is always on display: at work, with your family, strangers, or friends. Ask yourself these questions. What behaviors or energy do you bring to the world with your attitude, personality, characteristics, and honesty? How do you come across to others? Are you sharing your light and supporting the efforts of others through thoughtful and non-judgmental listening? Are you asking for support when you need it, giving others the opportunity to share their wisdom and compassion? People automatically want to help when they can. And you lending an ear is both a gift to you and to them.

Keeping your relationships peaceful and balanced are possible when you adjust your perceptions about who you are and what you're here to do, be, have, or learn. Using the Tools for Personal Growth should have given you some insight on that. How you show up in the world makes a statement about who you are ... a Spiritual being who is aligned with your Higher Power, not your typical self-absorbed ego.

It doesn't matter what position you hold, CEO or janitor, you'll most likely have some level of personality or ideology issues somewhere along the line. That's okay, as your position in life isn't so much about expressing your opinions and judgments. Showing up as your best self is about nurturing yourself and the relationships that contribute to everyone's inner peace and happiness.

Liberate your mind through your Spiritual practice (meditation) and the positive results must come back to liberate you from your fears, grievances, and judgments. Sometimes you just need to find quiet time to think through any issues that may be a block to your best self. Perceiving a situation from all angles can and will give you insight into how it can be made better. Just offer a little willingness and no matter how difficult or awkward it is, show up as your best self and you can't go wrong.

Tools for Your Personal Growth

Tool #1: Try to shift your mindset from ego-centered to Spirit-centered in every situation. That identity shift encourages you to show up in ways that reveal your light, not hide it.

Tool #2: Think of a situation that triggers a negative emotion in your mind. It might be something your teenager does or someone at work who demeans you. Take five minutes to rehearse that situation and see yourself reacting differently. Shift from anger to neutral. Shine your light on that person, not your darkness.

1.
2.
3.

Are You Projecting or Extending?

The Miracle-Minded believe that you are always either projecting or extending. To be more clear, when you're projecting (like a movie projector) you're putting/projecting your darkness, fears, or fault-finding onto someone else. You see the problem in that person, but it's really in you. Don't be offended because that person is there in front of you to show/reveal that to you. Here's a clue. You see in that person or situation what you are holding in your mind. Think of it as a wake up call.

To be extending is to be reaching out, like extending your hands outward, you're extending your light or kindness. To the Miracle-Minded it's a gesture of love. When you meet someone who is naturally kind, thoughtful, or caring … they are extending loving kindness.

By the same token, the Miracle-Minded believe that all outward expressions are *expressions of love or a call for love.* That might sound like a radical idea, but hear me out. If you meet someone who not kind or loving but is fearful, angry, or feeling threatened … it's actually a call for love! How is that handled? In this case, love is the answer. That's how to respond. To be more specific, you don't have to actually love that person, but be open to how you can help, understand, or support him/her. That's what they knowingly or unknowingly want from you.

Projecting at Work

Projecting also applies to your co-worker situations. Unhappy feelings at work are usually the result of stress, power plays (fear), workplace politics, poor management, and/or a basic dislike for the work or workplace environment.

Your co-workers may be having a similar experience and experience similar emotions. Angry or disappointing feelings are a call for love. Obvious bad energy calls for a talk with your human resource specialist or meeting in small groups to find solutions. To allow emotions to fester is destructive to small or large company morale and it goes downhill from there unless it's addressed. It's what we call "the elephant in the room," a big, bad situation that needs to be addressed.

A Tool for Your personal Growth

Ask yourself this question, *"Am I projecting my own insanity or am I extending my light & love?*

"Every mind must project or extend, because that is how it lives, and every mind is life." (ACIM: T7. 11.) (This quote means that every mind must either project its darkness or extend its light & love!)

Remove the Wall From Around Your Heart

I've invited you many times to look within, primarily for inner Guidance leading you to the people, places, and things of meaning to your Ideal Life Path. There's also the aspect of love, not intimate love, but what we think of as conventional or brotherly love ... the simple kindness that's unconditionally extended to everyone and everything. My sense of it is that if you don't extend or accept brotherly love, there's a metaphorical block wall around your heart.

If you look within during one of the personal growth tools/exercises and don't recognize your heart, it may be due to the wall surrounding it ... blocking it's light. Its natural state is to emanate light. ACIM says, *"you are the light of the world"* (ACIM: W-61) Your function is to shine your light as bright as possible. What is your light? It's your authenticity and your attitude, but it might also be your smile, kindness, compassion, gratitude, laughter, gentleness, or other displays of your innocence. There are ways to become aware of the blocks that hide your light and the love that is natural to you.

Later in this chapter you'll read about the process of mirroring and how it exposes your own internal blocks to the love within you and your brother/sister. Once you're aware of your blocks, you can take steps to heal them or at the very least diminish their effects on your relationships.

Some of the more general blocks to the awareness of love's presence or inner peace are constant grievances, anxiety, judgments, fear of not being enough, condemnation, jealousy, and a controlling personality. These blocks are ego-related and created over time due to lack of trust in who you really are and faith in your Higher Power. You can remove these blocks and other negativity by remembering all humans are Spiritual beings, not weakling creatures to be controlled, negated, or destroyed like bugs.

People may or may not sense your light, but I assure you they do sense your darkness. Be aware and open-minded about the negative traits such as judging another and holding grievances ... constant complaining. There is a workbook lesson in ACIM that says, *"My grievances hide the light of the world in me."* (ACIM: W-69) In other words, constant complaining hurts 'you' the most. We all know how difficult it is to stop finding fault in the world, especially when things are not to your liking. Do your best to look on the bright side.

*** **Truth**—I learned through personal experience that you can't follow your heart in all decisions unless you face the reality that your heart's wisdom and your truth are One. If you ignore your truth and what your heart is signaling to you, you'll be led astray. It may be a detour away from what you really want.

Think of times in your life when you didn't listen to your heart. You listened to someone else's demands, advice, or directions. Did that work for you? *

Shift from Fear to Love

I've talked about shifting from fear to love and how important it is to your own well-being, your relationships, and to your future. It all comes down to asking yourself how to thoughtfully handle difficult people and situations? Solutions about shifting perceptions are offered in the first few chapters of this book. Solutions will be different for you depending on your perceptions and situation.

Here are some questions to reflect on: Shifting From Fear to Love!

1. Would you rather be right or would you rather be happy?

2. What is the most loving thing to say or do in any situation?

3. Can you take a few minutes to go within, breathe, and speak from your heart (your truth)?

4. How would your Higher Power (Jesus, Buddha, the God of your heart or another benevolent Spirit Guide) perceive and respond to this situation?

A Tool for Your Personal Growth

Whatever is challenging you right now, stop and ask yourself the four questions about, *"Shifting from Fear to Love."* Sometimes the most loving thing you can do in a co-worker/employer situation is either speak your truth, quit, or move to another position in the company, if possible.

Think through your situation and choose a benevolent solution or discover a more mindful response. Look into your heart, think through the words of a wise person, and speak your words in a non-threatening way. Do your words or decision bring you peace?

This tool also applies to criminals or people who are a danger to themselves or society. The most loving thing you can do for them is to separate them from the people they may hurt or hurt them in return.

"When you meet anyone, it is a holy encounter, as you see him you will see yourself, as you treat him you will treat yourself." (ACIM: T-8.III)

Self-Healing Your Mind

With access to so many self-help and personal growth books written by experts, you may try to heal your mental and emotional symptoms on your own. Self-healing can be successful, especially if you have low levels of suffering.. It can be a simple matter of just making a different choice. You can make a big difference in your life by following simple directions, as you've read about in previous chapters. If you have serious issues and need to go deeper, an experienced counselor can help you through your pain, despair, or suffering.

Self-healing is possible if you are willing to work on yourself, be open-minded, and honest with yourself. It's critical to be disciplined in your approach, fair-minded, and not fall prey to your ego's need to be right.

Success comes from being adept at reviewing your former life situations and pain through a new lens ... the lens of love and compassion. You'll need to be strong to heal your suffering, misery, humiliation, or helplessness. This can be dangerous territory without a trained guide.

A Self-healing Visualization

First take your concerns to your Higher Power or inner Guide to get clarity and healing. If you aren't able to do that, I suggest several sessions with a trained counselor. Why is that necessary? When you go by yourself to a dark place in your mind, you may not have the training or background to save yourself from your misperceptions. There may be more to the story than you're telling yourself and there usually is. A trained therapist can help you with your misperceptions.

In a guided imagery session, your so-called enemy normally represents her or himself and their position with an explanation of *"a call for love."* That may cause you to perceive the situation differently than you did previously. There can be an unexpected outcome when you're open-minded, and it contributes to an understanding, healing, or resolution.

Do you run away from your problems? Moving to a different area, changing jobs, or quitting certain people doesn't solve anything. Understand the larger picture and you'll get a better conclusion. Regression and visualization with a trained counselor can help you clear your mind, heal your emotions, and allow your heart to speak its truth.

A counselor can assist you to align your heart and your understanding. Without it, you may find yourself in an abyss. In order to have a true healing, look at your past through a different lens, not as a victim, but as the victor. ACIM says, *"You're not a victim of the world you see."* (W-p1.31.) *"You are a victim of yourself and you can look at this differently."* (T-27.VlII.1O:1).

In the worst possible scenario you may go into your head, experience trauma, and not institute a healing. And that's what exploring your past is about ... not to wallow in the darkness, but to heal it and turn it into light. You know it's not easy, but shifting your perceptions is possible if you're willing. Leave the past in the past, and don't give it permission to muck up your present and future.

As it's summarized in ACIM: *"You are not trapped in the world you see, because its cause can be changed. This change requires, first, that the cause be identified and then [second] let go, so that [third] it can be replaced. The first two steps in this process require your cooperation. (with your Higher Power) The final one does not."* (W-p1.23.5:1-4).

Part Two: Tap Into Energetic Vibrations

Energetic Vibrations in Relationships

You've most likely experienced a personal energetic vibration from different people you've met. Some people seem to emit a good vibe and others ... not so much. There are different reasons for that and you'll explore some ideas that may explain why you get along with some people and not others.

The idea that relationships are all about energy is rooted in a holistic and metaphysical perspective on human interactions. It's holistically thought that every person and everything in the Universe emits and interacts with an energetic vibration or energy field surrounding them. It's not just about aligning horoscopes, moon signs, or holding back when "Mercury is in retrograde." Energies can be understood better from various perspectives, including psychological, emotional, and metaphysical.

An energetic connection can refer to the emotional and psychological connection between you, a family member, a co-worker, or stranger. The quality of interactions and the dynamics within your relationships are driven by the presence or absence of emotional connections or sometimes what you have in common. You eventually determine if that's enough to sustain it.

The Miracle-Minded are brought together with different people by their Higher Power for three different reasons. The first way might be a brief relationship to help with directions, knowledge, or something simplistic. Secondly, you and someone else are brought together for a short time, when each needs to learn lessons or something from the other. And the third reason is for a lifetime of personal growth experiences. And remember, there are no accidents in your Higher Power's plan for you. That person is there for a reason/season.

*** **Vibes and Atmosphere**—I attended a motivational event at a nearby conference center, so I was jazzed when I left. Afterwards I walked across the street to attend my friends' dinner party. I felt a big smile on my face and strong positive energy as I entered the room. I could tell people read that energy on me, as everyone wanted to talk to me. You can bring your good vibes and change the energy in a room full of people.*

Law of Attraction: You may be familiar with the law of attraction, a popular concept from metaphysics and personal development. It suggests that like attracts like. The LOA says that the energy you emit through your thoughts, emotions, and intentions may influence the type of people and relationships you attract. The LOA is beyond the scope of this book. You may search for books and videos on this popular topic.

Energetic Resonance: Resonance is the idea that people with similar energies or frequencies are naturally drawn to each other and can quite possibly form deeper, more meaningful connections. When you resonate on an emotional and energetic level, you tend to understand each other better and have stronger bonds. This resonance can create a sense of connection, understanding, and harmony.

Emotional Contagion: Research in psychology has shown that emotions can be contagious. When one person in a relationship experiences a strong emotion, it can influence the emotions of others in the relationship, such as a family. For example, if one person is consistently anxious or angry, it can affect the overall emotional energy of the relationship. It works the same way when the more influential person is happy and carefree, affecting everyone in a small workplace.

Communication: Communication in relationships is not just about words but also about the emotional energy that goes along with those words. You may emit nonverbal cues like a kind tone of voice, welcoming body language, and pleasant facial expressions that impact your message to others.

Well-Being: Positive and supportive relationships can enhance mental and emotional health, while negative or toxic relationships can lead to stress and unhappiness. You'll no doubt feel these energies as you regularly interact with co-workers at your workplace.

Empathy and Intuition: Some people believe that empathy and intuition are manifestations of a particular energetic awareness. Empathy is the ability to understand and share the feelings of another person, especially if you have the ability to sense and connect with their energy.

Healing and Balance: Healing and maintaining healthy relationships involve balancing and harmonizing your own energy and that of the relationship. Techniques like meditation, energy work, and mindfulness are usually recommended to achieve this balance.

Interconnectedness: This perspective emphasizes the interconnectedness of all living beings. It suggests that our energies are not isolated but interconnected with the energies of others and the Universe as a whole.

This holistic perspective on energetic relationships is not scientifically proven and is mainly associated with metaphysical beliefs, although I believe personal experience is the best teacher. You may find value in the idea of energetic vibrations in relationships or not. Use it if it helps you in any way.

Decisions, Intuition, and Emotions: I believe there's a strong connection between your intuition, emotions, and your decision-making processes. Because emotions are involved, it's not always subtle. It can be a rocky ride.

Intuition is like a whisper or nudge from your inner wisdom, guiding you through life's twists and turns, ins and outs. It speaks to you in subtle and sometimes not so subtle ways, often through your emotions. Your emotions are powerful messengers, signaling to you what resonates with your deepest desires and values, and what doesn't. When you're faced with questions or important decisions, your intuition tunes into these emotional signals, helping you navigate towards what aligns with your authentic self.

Think of intuition as a finely tuned instrument that picks up on the vibrations of your emotions. When you're considering a choice or facing a dilemma, your intuition might send you feelings of excitement, joy, or peace if the path aligns with your true purpose. Alternately, it might send signals of discomfort, unease, or tension if something doesn't quite fit.

For instance, imagine you're contemplating a job offer. Logically, it seems like a great opportunity, but there's a nagging feeling in your gut that something isn't quite right. That's your intuition at work, tapping into your emotions to alert you to potential red flags or incongruence's with your values.

Your emotions are a rich source of information, often revealing insights that your rational mind might overlook. Intuition helps you decipher these emotional cues, guiding you towards choices that resonate with your deeper truth. It's like having a compass within you, pointing you towards your North Star—the path that leads to fulfillment, growth, and authenticity. By cultivating awareness of your emotions and learning to trust your intuition, you can tap into a profound source of guidance and wisdom.

This doesn't mean dismissing logic or reason, but rather integrating them with your intuitive insights to make more aligned and fulfilling decisions in life. As you practice listening to the nudges of your intuition, you strengthen your connection to your inner guidance system, empowering you to navigate life with greater clarity, purpose, and authenticity.

*** **Honor Your Emotions**—The decision making process is important and decision makers will do well to take a holistic view of decision-making: Spirit, Mind, and Body. Being guided by Spirit in a decision matter is the best and easiest way. When you don't or can't connect with Spirit, then the ego mind has its way with you. This means taking into account what your mind tells you, which is typically analytic, common sense, or an ego approach. The body then reads those vibrations and taps into your emotions, *"How do I really feel about that decision?"* And your emotions get to feel joy, cry, or shout.

I was invited to a wedding at a distant location and I agreed to participate. As I searched for flights, hotels, and tourist events I realized there were a number of personal reasons I should not attend. I asked but received no Guidance. And yet I still felt an attraction to the event and a location I loved so long ago. I held off making reservations due to the mental and emotional conflict of choosing to go or not. I was on the verge of cancelling when I felt stuck in the conflict, like it was thick, heavy mud.

Over the next week I stayed with my feelings of whether I should go or not? The thought of cancelling just didn't feel right and I instinctively knew I needed to look at my personal reasons without bias or negativity. The instant I made my reservations peace replaced the torture I had been feeling and the struggle disappeared.*

Part Three: Be Miracle-Minded in Your Relationships

Co-workers, Friends, and Family, Oh My!

You can call this solution: *"Tigers, Lions, and Bears, Oh My!"* Dorothy and her friends in the movie, The Wizard of Oz, came across many dangers on their journey to meet the all-powerful wizard. They were told he could help them get a heart, courage, a brain and a way back Home. Having a brave heart, endless courage, an aware mind, and a desire to reach Home are all required on this Spiritual journey. Your wizard is not hiding behind a curtain, but is within you… your inner Guide. Your intimate life journey may include co-workers, friends, and family who are possible bridges to you living your truth and happiness.

Discover and help them get what they need from your inner Guidance. Be a bridge to others.

According to your Higher Power through *A Course in Miracles,* your real purpose in life is to know *who you really are* in order to heal and forgive your unhealed relationships; with yourself and the people you interact with. When you know who YOU are, you'll know who OTHERS are ... they're just like you!

It may seem like a tall order because relationships can be challenging on many levels. It doesn't have to be difficult, but a fair amount of letting go (of your ego needing to be right) is required. This calls for a larger amount of willingness. Remember that the letting go and willingness part are for your benefit and peace first.

Your part in your relationships, as one who is Miracle-Minded, is to shift your thinking from fear to love. Let up on the attitude and remember that ego centered or fearful thinking by anyone is a call for love—whether it's you or someone else. The best response is a *return of love* to that person's call. Responding to someone's *call for love* can be as simple as a sweet smile, a kind word, a friendly nod, or a vote of confidence. Your awareness will help tone down any drama in your life instead of perpetuating it.

If you are the more sane person in the drama, and are Miracle-Minded, it's up to you to break the cycle of insanity by bringing an element of peace and sensibility to your situation. Keep it real and speak from your heart!

Readjusting your halo is about shifting your perceptions about what your relationships and the world are for ... to allow love and peace to flow freely so everyone experiences Happiness Now!

"Kindness is an emotional act of abundance. To show your kindness or love to another does not mean less for someone else."

Difficult Bosses

No doubt there are difficult-to-deal-with superiors that you may have to answer to or share space with every day. In fact, you may be that difficult person, so this chapter applies to you also. The difficult ones include people who may be somewhat incompetent, narcissistic, or perhaps insecure due to a fragile ego. That person may be a demanding micromanager. He or she might exhibit abusive, emotionally antagonistic, or sexually demanding behavior.

If you put yourself in the other person's shoes you may have a better understanding of what drives them to be as they are. And yet there are never reasons to abuse your co-worker. You have no idea of what that person is dealing with from their superiors, the Board, or investors. A difficult person may also have issues at home with their family, with their health, from their past, with their emotions, or finances. Nor do they know what you're dealing with on a daily basis.

Some people may not see eye to eye with you and may be difficult to get along with. They may see you and your ambitions or your light as a threat. Honest communication and heart to heart talks are often the way to better relationships.

*** **Letting go**—Laura worked for a project manager at a small company. It became clear to her the manager wanted her out so personal friends could take over her position. As her counselor, I was told the manager blamed many errors on her because she didn't speak the manager's particular language. Speaking another language was not a requirement when Laura was hired. The manager was hired a year later than Laura and used her superior position to make Laura's life miserable. She emotionally bullied Laura during the private weekly meetings she insisted upon. Laura felt her superior was unfit to be a manager and would have liked the opportunity to give a performance review. Of course that didn't happen. The last time I saw Laura for a counseling session she felt hurt by the emotional abuse but let it go and was happy to move on.*

Daily Stress

As in the example above, you may have daily stress that eats away at your inner peace, goals, and confidence. You may have a strong work ethic and are susceptible to overwhelm. Stress eventually leads to physical pain if its not addressed. Daily stress can be handled through the relaxation response of meditation, mindfulness, and breath work.

Sometimes people take on a lucrative management position and later quit the position due to stress. Their prior position was more comfortable. The stress level should always be part of the decision making process when choosing to leave or stay in a career or work situation.

Relationships as Mirrors

The idea of mirroring is a timeless and productive process that raises your awareness of the ego self. This simple practice can open the door: to a better understanding of yourself and why some relationships are so difficult. They exist to show you a better way!

*** **Your Gift**—Self-awareness was a tough lesson for Jack, who shared his frustration in a counseling session. He had a problem with one of his teachers who he perceived as angry, selfish, and controlling. It was easy for him to perceive those dark traits in another person.

After I explained how mirroring works, Jack was open-minded enough to do a test. He made a list of those nasty traits that always made him angry. Once he studied the list of his teachers' dark traits and mined his own past/emotions, he realized that he also had those traits. Jack discovered the process was accurate and his teacher was mirroring back to Jack his own dark traits. Otherwise, how would he know had them? He initially didn't want to see himself in people he disliked. It's initially not a pleasant discovery. Is that a gift? It could be if he would take steps to make corrections by becoming less angry, selfish, and controlling. Or he could go through life butting up against people just like his teacher and himself.*

Co-create the Best Version of Yourself

Like Jack, you'll want to project your best self to others as you either heal past relationships or step onto your new life path. A new and positive mindset may be required for the next part of your journey.

A graphic designers' mindset is very different from that of a small business owner, an administrative assistant, a cooking school teacher, or a non-fiction writer. No matter which life path you take, you'll either build relationships, muck them up, or move on from them. Mirroring is a good way to perceive behaviors that don't build relationships or camaraderie.

Once you turn that mirror onto yourself, you'll most likely see your own neuroses. Jack learned to see his own traits mirrored in another: anger, selfishness, and needing to control people around him. Jack thought of his teacher as his enemy, but was he really? A different attitude and perception might reveal that his teacher was actually his savior.

Apply this process to your own disturbing relationships. Be open-minded, let go of your anger, and accept what that person is showing you. Take notice of how that makes you feel and how you might heal your own negativity by watching your thoughts like a hawk. Correct them when they start to go south. Is there a lesson to be learned from the experience? The Miracle-Minded know it's not your place to change someone else. It's your place to make a correction in your own attitude and/or behavior.

Through mirroring, you've been given the awareness of the negative traits that hide your light and keep love away. Your Spirit is perfect, but you're here on this Earth school to per-fect' your human self i.e. your ego mind, and that's how it's done. Always check with your Higher Power for additional guidance.

As one who is Miracle-Minded, you would remind yourself to move away from your ego-dum thinking by doing the opposite of what you've previously done. To dissolve anger; be calm and think before you speak. Will attacking that person really accomplish anything other than satisfying your ego? Probably not! To prevent selfishness; be more vigilant about how open-minded, generous, and kind you are toward sharing with others.

ACIM says, *"To give and to receive are one in truth."* (ACIM: W-119)

Letting go of control issues is to let go of your need to be right! *"Do you prefer that you be right or happy?"* (ACIM: T-29.VII) To always make someone else wrong is to dishonor them and contribute to uncomfortable feelings. Can you solve disagreements in a way that is harmonious?

Once you make those changes, you'll be seen in a more positive light. Here's the best part ... you won't run across those negative traits in other people because you've healed those parts of yourself. They're no longer visible in the other person nor in you.

You may not know someone who is honest enough to point out your faults (maybe your mother?), and ego controllers may not believe it anyway. The Universe comes through for you by placing someone directly in front of you to show you just how ugly those ego-dum traits can be. That's the beauty of co-creating with the Universe.

Attract More Love and Friendships

Mirroring can help you learn the causes that keep love/friendship away. You want to attract more love, kindness, and friendship, not push it away. Now you have a short list and you know if another persons' dark traits cause you upset, then your traits most likely affect others in a similar way.

For example, you understand that your own dark traits are anger, selfishness, and being a control freak (or whatever yours are?). Realize that all negative ego-dum traits fall under the umbrella of fear!

- Ask yourself, *"What am I afraid of?"*
- What are the benefits of continuing to express these negative traits?

- How may these traits undermine the achievement of your Dreams?
- What thoughts and perceptions can shift these traits?
- Where do you go from here?

There are ways to heal negative traits once you know what they are:
- Stop and think before you speak. Are your words positive and thoughtful?
- Stay away from judgments. Can you approach matters in a neutral way?
- Let go of the past. Start a new chapter without bringing past hurts along?
- Remember how insults or derogatory behaviors hurt you in the past. Compassion is always the right emotion.

To attract more love and friendships is to invite your Higher Power into your next meditation or before you sleep to help you with your anger issues. Share your feelings and your willingness to shift your emotions.

Secondly, education is another way. There are classes in anger management. Anger comes from not being able to control things the way you want. Learn to let go, like my stallion story in Chapter Five entitled *Surrender*, or compromise with a win/win solution. Step back, pause, think, and speak wisely!

Selfishness is a trait that can be averted through mindfulness. Be more generous or put others first when you can. Showing you care about others' feelings and needs demonstrates a kind heart and compassionate attitude. That's who you really are and it's a valuable insight.

Most of us are addicted to control in one way or another and it's like telling your Higher Power that you don't need it. You are in control! Stepping back is one way to break the cycle of control. Practicing mindfulness and letting go are two more ways to heal your control issues. Allow people to be who they are, just as they allow you to be who you are. Step back and know others are consciously or unconsciously following their own hearts. Free those you try to control from your mental prison.

SUCCESS SKILLS

The two success skills for this solution are: *open-mindedness and letting go*. Practice both of these skills on a regular basis and you have discovered the quickest way to become Miracle-Minded.

Tools for Your Personal Growth

Tool #1: Choose one or two people in your workplace who you find challenging. Make a short list for each one describing what you perceive as their faults. Give each person at least five minutes of your attention. Be aware if any of their perceived faults apply to you? Mine your interactions with them and be as honest as possible.

Tool #2: Take those negative traits/blocks to your inner Guide in your next meditation/prayer to learn how they can best be healed. Keep trying if you don't get an answer right away. Look at those negative traits or faults again and ask yourself: *"what can I let go of?" "How will letting go help my relationship?" "Will letting go still allow me to be happy?"*

Tool #3: Show those people you may have slighted that you're a better person than you were yesterday. These are easy traits to change if your intention is to make honest changes in a compassionate and harmonious way. What negative traits could you eliminate to help you become your best self?

*** **A Miracle**—Pauline shared this story of her former work place. You'll learn how seeming enemies from a corporate culture may become friends. She and her former co-workers meet once a month to have dinner together in various restaurants around town. She shared how everyone has a good time: laughing, eating together, sharing stories of their children, grandchildren, travels, and a relaxed retirement. Most people never miss a group lunch due to the joy they experience.

She then explained how this same group of co-workers who are now retired, disabled, laid off, or quit used to behave at their corporate job. They argued, complained, didn't get along, and pretty much hated each other.

In a way it was a shocking story that they could finally come together in joy and harmony ... that time and distance was the healer of those now forgotten wounds. The problems may also have been stress, power struggles, workplace politics, and a basic dislike for their work in an industrial setting. The miracle in this situation was that they remembered what they did like about each other and finally gave precedence to those characteristics. *

*** **A Sweet Melody**—Will also tells a story of his group of co-workers who worked together harmoniously. Many years after retirement they still meet for their once-a-month retirement lunches. He reports the same good vibrations that always existed.*

* These two stories of different workplace cultures show how healing can take place when people are either forgiving of past errors in judgment or left the judgment game off the table once and for all.

SUCCESS SKILLS

The Success Skills to learn are honesty with yourself, mindfulness, and letting go. A challenging co-worker or family member doesn't need to know they're your mirror. They may find the idea insulting. It's their role to show you how you hide your light behind a wall of darkness.

A Tool for Your Personal Growth

Who from your past are you ready to forgive? Can you see them differently?

1.
2.
3.

Part Four—Be Miracle-Minded for Freedom

Discover Your Entryway to Happiness Now

One thing is crystal clear to the Miracle-Minded. It's that relationships and forgiveness are like a horse and carriage. Each one is more valuable or useful with the other. Relationships and forgiveness represents a small or large entryway into your total freedom.

You'll be your happiest when the entryway opens and your relationships are peaceful and without conflict. They're that important! The people in your life can be critical resources and supporters. Ignoring their value to your current life, Dream, or purpose detracts from their significance. To celebrate your achievements without supportive friends etc. is a lonely and unfulfilling endgame.

Some Spiritual travelers will be guided to follow and support you and your Ideal Life Path. You'll be brought together by Divine intervention. You may have a small percentage of dear friends who support you in your creative endeavors or your small business. Others may only enjoy your friendship and conversation.

There is a popular quote by the late motivational speaker Zig Ziglar, who said, *"You can get everything you want in life by helping enough other people get what they want."* That idea is an unspoken transactional promise. That's how many relationships work.

That's why it's so important to know what you want so you can ask for it from those who are capable of providing it to you. And you'll do the same for them. Happiness is contagious ... pass it on!

Forgiveness and Freedom = Happiness Now!

The most beneficial inner power is experienced when you choose to let go of your grievances. Forgive and release the people and situations you think, *"Wronged you, broke your heart, or stepped on your toes."* Give them and yourself the gift of FREEDOM!

The entryway to happiness and freedom is a forgiving perspective: Idolizing your emotional wounds doesn't heal them. It keeps them alive and unhealed. Refrain from crucifying yourself over and over! It's not worth the stress, despair, or dis-ease to hold onto a situation from the past that's over and is now meaningless. It doesn't matter if it's the men or women in your life, former co-workers, teachers, parents, or even yourself. It's time to move on and take your power back from your ego-dum. Apply that energy to helping yourself be a more enlightened, awakened, and forgiving hero.

A Course In Miracles has a more radical way of looking at freedom and happiness as well as past, present, and future events. It asks you to let go of the past because it's no longer there. It can keep you from joyfully living your life in the present moment. ACIM says when you think of the past your mind is actually blank. It's the same when you think about the future. Clearly, ACIM directs you to stay in the present moment allowing your inner Guide to lead you in the present to a future of it's own making ... the will of your Higher Power.

When you think of your mind as blank, you have the option of co-creating what you and Spirit would have it be. You are free to look at your past differently and to reframe or behold a past that frees you from any pain or trauma. Reframe your past situation in a way that allows you to become the victor instead of the victim. By the same token you'll co-create in the present what will come to be your future.

*** **Skeletons**—While writing this book I had a dream about a former childhood friend. I hadn't seen her since my family moved away from our former neighborhood when I was about fourteen years of age. In the dream I came across her, as an adult, near our former hometown. I was friendly and asked, "Hello, how are you?" She just stared straight into my eyes without saying a word. That tiny interaction left me with an uncomfortable feeling, and I sensed that she wasn't going to respond, so I walked away. In that moment of 'the stare' I felt as if her hurt or whatever she was feeling had been psychically transferred to my mind, heart, and soul.

In my awareness I immediately remembered two incidents from our childhood where, looking back, could be perceived as thoughtless or hurtful on my part. Was that upsetting her? Had she not forgiven me? I really didn't know since I haven't seen her in many years. Of course, I regret whatever resentment she might still feel toward me after all these years. My actions then were not intentional, but perhaps immature, selfish, and thoughtless. I can't possibly know what she felt then that bothered her or how she processed those incidents. She never mentioned them. And the possibility remains that I overreacted to the dream.

I can't change the past or take away her experience but I felt her pain and the guilt and shame of my own thoughtless actions. Perhaps that was her soul's intention … to reveal how unconscious childhood actions have repercussions? Her haunting stare awakened me to that fact and I can do something about my part in it. I can feel remorse, and heal my past thoughtlessness by remembering that I too am flawed. I continue to work on myself to become a better person who would not behave so recklessly.

Also, the skeletons who have come back to haunt me can be buried in a bed of forgiveness. Whether she has forgiven me or not is up to her and if so, she can choose to free both of us. Regardless of her decision, I can't change the past, but I could forgive myself for my past errors and remember my holy innocence.*

Suffering is Not an Option

Like myself, you may have suffered due to the thoughtless actions or inactions of others, as well as those you've mindlessly perpetrated. I've also suffered at the hands of former relationships. I've experienced both ends of the stick; the sharp point that hurts others and the sharpness of the other end jabbed at me. It's never easy to get over it or let it go and yet our Higher Power encourages us to free ourselves and others … and let it rest!

As children and also as adults we do hurtful or selfish things to others without thinking of another's feelings. We're doing what we've learned from misguided peers, movies, or television. On some level our society and our ego trains us to take care of #1. This is your Higher Power's Kingdom, which means it's not *"everyone for himself"* or *"you and me against the world."* That's just BS! As Alexandre Dumas, author of *The Three Musketeers* wrote, *"It's All for One and One for all!"*

"Forgiveness is my function as the Light of the World"(ACIM: W-62)

A Course in Miracles and the Miracle-Minded are very clear that forgiveness is the key to happiness! To forgive yourself and others establishes your own little personal world as light-filled and free rather than a dark hellhole ... by not holding grievances against yourself or another. By forgiving, letting go, or overlooking the error, you are demonstrating that you are a being of light, not darkness. It establishes the truth of who you really are ... a holy and blessed Spiritual being having a human experience.

Remember that you're not forgiving to 'do that person a favor,' you're forgiving to free each other from the chains that bind you together in darkness for all time.

You can think of forgiveness as a gift to yourself. There should be no doubt in your mind that forgiving yourself or another is an act of strength, courage, and the power of the Christ Consciousness within you. (If you aren't a believer in Christ consciousness, feel free to substitute your own wording for that term.) Forgiveness is a gift that lives on in you as your brother or sister's savior and has the potential to change the consciousness of the world.

There is a popular prayer for the Miracle-Minded in the book, ACIM. Use it whenever you are not joyous:

"I must have decided wrongly, because I am not at peace.

I made the decision myself, but I can also decide otherwise.

I want to decide otherwise, because I want to be at peace.

I do not feel guilty, because the Holy Spirit will undo all the consequences of my wrong decision if I will let Him.

I choose to let Him, by allowing Him to decide for God for me."

(ACIM -T-5.VII.6:7-1 1)

"Your investment in anger and guilt is undone and replaced by the Love of God ... the final step in your healing." (ACIM: T-3.IV)

Claim a More Powerful Identity

A more powerful identity is waiting for you. Shift your perception of who you are at your core and choose to follow your inner light. You know your Divinity when you display kindness, laughter, and gentleness. The Miracle-Minded know that you may self identify as whatever you want, but your self-identity as Spirit is the most powerful.

Outcomes:

* Choose Spirit Identification and you gain personal power through your intuition, creativity, and imagination.

* Choose Spirit Identification and align with your Higher Power's will for you.

* Choose Spirit Identification and you have your Higher Power (The God of your heart, the Universe, or the Divine) and Spirit Guides, Angels, and Heavenly Helpers to assist you on your Ideal Life Path and in your relationships.

* Choose Spirit Identification to live a life of happiness, and fulfillment.

* *Spiritual law says you cannot serve two Masters.* Which will you choose?

Got A Problem?

This section is an important part of the thought system of the Miracle-Minded. Got a problem? There's only one solution. The Miracle-Minded know that you have only one problem and that is *separation from your Higher Power*. A belief and feelings of separation is the cause of fearful and negative thoughts. It would be the reason you have faulty perceptions.

Any hopelessness or despair is proof that you believe in the separation, that you believe your Higher Power doesn't love you or is not caring for you in your life. You might think your connection to the Divine is broken or you're guilty of something and He's abandoned you. You've been told through a faulty belief system that you're being punished and in some circles it's called 'sin.' Nothing could be further from the truth! To sin means to *miss the mark*. The Miracle-Minded will assure you that you've made an error, a mistake, and mistakes are to be corrected and forgiven. The better thought is that, because of who you are (a Spirit having a human experience), you are always forgiven and asked to forgive others as you are freed from your mistakes. The only solution is to heal the separation through unity: align and connect with your Higher Power.

ACIM says, *"God does not forgive because He has never condemned."* (ACIM:W-46) With that idea, fear of a wrathful God is gone. In essence you're freed from what you thought you did or didn't do. This is, to our world, a radical idea that could bring about real change.

Let go of your fear and separation to feel confident about the Spirit you really are. As you shift your perceptions and continue to forgive yourself and others, you'll free yourself and others from the bondage of judgment and condemnation.

Never hide from your inner light and who you really are ... a beloved child of your Higher Power (God/the Divine). You are free to step into your HAPPINESS NOW life.

Part Five—Empower Yourself

Utilize Your Superpowers

Storytellers focus on superpowers such as magic/ synchronicity, inner strength, insight, or an unexpected and surprising creative power within. They are all natural superpowers you may be capable of when you believe in yourself, free up your belief system, and are self-aware enough to realize the holy truth inside you.

You've read my personal stories and how I was able to experience mind-boggling synchronicities, surprising inner strength, unusual insights, and unlimited creative potential. That's just the tip of the iceberg.

Digging deep for the truth inside you is what this search and discovery mission is all about. Do you want to learn who you are, who you're meant to be, to do or to have? It's your Higher Power's will for you to have that realization. Course correcting and building a personal foundation of success skills are key.

There are Success Skills I consider to be superpowers. Some of these are mindfulness, letting go, honesty, patience, listening, being grounded, faith, focus, clarity, integrity, and your imagination. On some level utilizing these success skills are your Ideal Life Path. Learning them and grounding yourself propels you forward in whatever direction you go in life.

* *"Let go of your story so the Universe can write a new one for you."* online quote—Marianne Williamson, best selling author & U.S. Presidential Candidate

Tell Yourself a Different Story

Everyone has their own unique story of what they've lived through on this planet ... their successes and failures, adventures, and misadventures. Whatever your story is, you can change direction or deepen your direction starting now.

Whether you're ready to live your Ideal Life Path or continue with an uncomfortable existence, you can choose to live a story that pleases you. It might be a story of purpose, peace, and love. You might choose a story of confidence, prosperity, and abundance. Or you could live a story of kindness, compassion, and forgiveness. It's your story and you're encouraged and entitled to co-create your heart's desire!

Pick and choose the super powers you want to wield in the world and use them when given the opportunity to choose. As always, you can choose from your ego or your Spirit, and your powers that be will arise in conjunction with that choice.

A Tool for Personal Growth

Imagine that you are at the end of your life. What story will you tell about yourself?

Your Next Steps

Forgiveness is total freedom: for yourself, co-workers, family, and friends. It means everything to the achievement of your future happiness.

*** **Author's Afterward:** I don't live with the regret, *"I wish I had done more with my life,"* because a dream forewarned me of this wish. That dream set me off on a life-changing journey to more adventures and personal growth than I could ever write about. I've enjoyed almost every minute of everything I've ever done. Sure, there were glitches in the continuum but I got through it and moved on to better things. It takes courage and on many levels I've let go of fear and so can you.

Once you awaken to clearly hearing the Voice for God, you know you're being guided along your Life Purpose. You can trust that you are connected, aligned, and loved beyond measure, as you've always been. Popular personal growth experts provided me with their valuable Spiritual teachings and the knowledge to go deeper with Spirit. I've passed on my own personal lessons and experiences to you in the form of this memoir and Miracle-Minded coaching program. I shared my Process of Discovery and the three careers that attracted my interest in midlife: writer, culinarian, and artist. I chose the one that had the most meaning for me, a writer who ended up living in the very expensive San Francisco Bay Area, who could possibly make a difference in the world.The point I want to make, as I previously said, the Universe always says, *"yes!"* An outsider looking in might ask, *"Which one of the three options is your Ideal Life Path?"* I believe it could be all of them or even none of them. It doesn't really matter. The experiences did what they were supposed to do. They enriched my life in more ways than I could count, as each of your choices will do for you ... if you look at them as steppingstones to a life of purpose and joy. *Thanks for coming on this journey with me!*

From my heart to yours,

Linda

Please visit me at:

www.LearnYourLifePurpose.com

or

www.HeartToHeartLiving.com

www.ingramcontent.com/pod-product-compliance
Lightning Source LLC
Chambersburg PA
CBHW071707090426
42738CB00009B/1696